Learning Resource Centre

Park Road, Uxbridge, Middlesex UB8 1NQ
Renewals: 01895 853344

UXBRIDGE
COLLEGE

Decades of our Lives

90s

Decades of our Lives

CLASSIC, RARE, AND UNSEEN

90s

FROM THE ARCHIVES OF THE DAILY MAIL

Trans
Atlantic
Press

Introduction

The fall-out from the Soviet Union's disintegration dominated European politics in the last decade of the millennium. There were winners and losers as former Communist states embraced free-market economics, but the greatest strife followed the fragmentation of Yugoslavia. Serbia's desire to prevent Bosnia, Croatia, Slovenia, and Macedonia from going their own way sparked a bloody Balkan conflict. Saddam Hussein was also on the march, Iraq's invasion of Kuwait ended by the Allied forces and Desert Storm. Baghdad took a pounding but Saddam lived to fight another day. There was genocide in Rwanda, an uprising in Chechnya and a humanitarian crisis in Somalia. Dunblane, Columbine, and Waco were scenes of carnage, Omagh and Oklahoma fell victim to bomb outrages. Mandela went from prisoner to president, Germany was reunited and

Britain joined Europe via the "Chunnel"—but baulked at adopting its new currency. America and Britain took a leftward step with Clinton and Blair. Neither "Zippergate" nor impeachment could dent "Slick Willie's" popularity. Britons rioted over the Poll Tax, worried about catching "mad cow" disease and mourned the death of Diana. "Posh and Becks" took over as the golden couple, and we could read about them on the internet as well as in celebrity columns. We had Britpop, Britart, *Friends* and *The Simpsons*. Tiger chalked up his first major, "Pistol Pete" ruled the tennis court, and Lance Armstrong beat cancer and cycling's finest to win the Tour. From the momentous and the apocalyptic to the offbeat and the trivial, the photographs in this book, from the archives of the *Daily Mail*, chart the people, places and events that made up a memorable decade.

1990

RIGHT: On February 11, 1990 at 2:10 P.M., crowds celebrated as the news of Nelson Mandela's release flashed around the world. Mandela had been imprisoned for 27 years after being charged with sabotage and other crimes committed during his fight against the apartheid system. Throughout his sentence there was international pressure to release him and finally after F.W. de Clerk became president of South Africa and reversed the ban on anti-apartheid movements, Mandela's freedom was granted. He immediately resumed his leadership of the ANC and led multi-party negotiations to achieve the first multi-racial elections in the country.

OPPOSITE: Mandela pictured two months after his release as he visited the wife of Oliver Tambo. Tambo, a member of the ANC and close friend of Mandela had lived in London for 30 years gathering support against apartheid, but returned to South Africa in 1991 where he became National Chairperson of the ANC. He died in 1993.

1990

LEFT: Jodie Foster pictured in 1990, two years after winning her first Academy Award for Best Actress in *The Accused*. In January 1991, the movie that would give her a second Oscar and the role for which she was most famous, *Silence of the Lambs,* broke quietly but accumulated great critical praise for Foster and co-star Anthony Hopkins who also won Best Actor. Foster would also step out in her directorial debut with *Little Man Tate* in 1991.

OPPOSITE: Jodie Foster, as Clarice Starling, faces Hannibal Lecter, played by Anthony Hopkins, in the chilling movie based on Thomas Harris's novel, *Silence of the Lambs*, in production in 1990. The menace of Lecter and the controlled calm of Starling give a unique dimension of terror that is felt by the audience all the way through the film.

1990

The World Cup semi-final between West Germany and England was goalless until a free kick from Andreas Brehme was deflected past England's goalkeeper Peter Shilton in the 60th minute. With 10 minutes left Gary Lineker equalized for England, forcing extra-time. England's Paul Gascoigne received his second yellow card of the competition and, in perhaps the most iconic moment of the tournament, openly wept at the realization that he would not be allowed to play in the final if England were to advance. However, West Germany progressed to the final winning the penalty shoot-out, 4–3.

The West German football team celebrate with the World Cup trophy, having defeated Argentina 1–0 in the final held in Rome. The winning goal was scored from the penalty spot in the 85th minute by Andreas Brehme, in an aggressively contested game that saw Argentina have two men sent off—a first for a World Cup Final. On a more positive note, West Germany's victory ensured that manager Franz Beckenbauer became just the second man to have lifted the cup as both a player and a coach.

1990

ABOVE: On January 31, 1990 McDonald's opened its first ever restaurant in Russia. Overwhelmed by demand to taste the delicacy brought to Russia at the end of the Soviet era, McDonald's struggled to keep up with Muscovites standing in long lines to enter the busiest and biggest McDonald's restaurant in the world, sited in Pushkin Square, Moscow. McDonald's received over 25,000 applications to work in the new branch.

OPPOSITE: American model and actress Jerry Hall pictured in burlesque costume. A successful model since the mid-1970s, in 1990 Hall featured in Roger Waters' all-star production of *The Wall live in Berlin*. The show was staged close to the site of the Berlin Wall, which had begun to be officially dismantled that summer. Later in the year Hall was to marry long-time love interest Mick Jagger on the Indonesian island of Bali.

OPPOSITE: Rock star Prince on stage during 1990's Nude tour, which saw Prince and his recently rearranged backing band performing a stripped-down live show. This effectively amounted to a "greatest hits" set, and included such songs as "1999," "Kiss," and "Purple Rain," although new compositions such as "Thieves in the Temple," from Prince's movie *Graffiti Bridge*, were also included. The 1990 film proved to be a flop, although the soundtrack LP was highly successful.

RIGHT: Fashion designer and activist Vivienne Westwood, probably the most important creative force behind the look of the 1980s punk movement, shows she hasn't lost her playful spirit when she joins a picket line at the Natural History Museum, London, sporting a fig leaf.

LEFT: Monica Seles won the 1990 French Open at the age of just 16 and achieved women's world number one ranking for 1991–92. Seen here playing at Wimbledon, Seles got no further than the quarter-final. Her career suffered a major setback when she was stabbed by one of the crowd at a match in Hamburg in 1993; the man, wielding a 10-inch knife was obsessed with Steffi Graf and considered Seles a threat. Monica retired from the international tennis circuit for two years.

OPPOSITE: Croatian tennis player Goran Ivanisevic in action at Wimbledon in 1990. Having turned professional just two years earlier, Ivanisevic caused something of a stir in 1990 by defeating Boris Becker in the first round of the French Open, although Becker would beat him in the Wimbledon semi-finals later in the year.

1990

OPPOSITE: Prime Minister Margaret Thatcher was faced with poor ratings in the opinion polls and in November 1990 the resignation of her deputy, Geoffrey Howe, over European Union policy further undermined her position. Days later backbencher Michael Heseltine challenged her for the leadership of the Conservative Party and in the following contest, Mrs. Thatcher resigned to avoid defeat. It was John Major who received her support and won the leadership contest. Honored with the Order of Merit by the Queen in 1990, she received a life peerage after retiring from the House of Commons in 1992.

RIGHT: British Fashion Model Paula Hamilton was discovered by photographer David Bailey and rose to fame in the 1980s after featuring in the "Changes" television commercial for Volkswagen. Although her career was affected by battles against drug and alcohol addiction, she continued to work during the 1990s, notably appearing in Take That's music video for the 1996 single, "How Deep is Your Love."

1990

RIGHT: The 1979 Conservative Party election manifesto promised reforms to local taxes; the resulting Community Charge legislation was due for implementation on April 1, 1990. Despite vociferous opposition, prime minister Margaret Thatcher refused to back down on what was known as the "Poll Tax." On March 31 around 200,000 protesters marched on Trafalgar Square and in the late afternoon, as the rally was coming to an end, violence broke out in the crowds, initiating "The Battle of Trafalgar." The ensuing riot was the largest civil disturbance seen in the capital in the 20th century, and resulted in thousands of injuries, hundreds of arrests, and massive damage to property, including the burning and looting of businesses and cars. This bitter message to the government was the first step in Thatcher's decline from power.

ABOVE: A protester launches a wooden stave through the window of a police car.

1990

OPPOSITE: Berliners wave German flags in front of the Brandenburg Gate as they celebrate the country's reunification. The Iron Curtain, the division between East and West Europe, started to crumble in 1989 when Hungary began to open its borders. East Germany soon followed suit by relaxing border restrictions and on October 3, 1990, Germany was finally reunited.

LEFT: The Strangeways Prison riots began in Manchester on April 1, 1990. Inmates initially took control of the chapel, after a Sunday morning service, before seizing the whole building. Tensions were peaking and prisoners felt their grievances were being ignored. After long negotiations the siege ended 25 days later but the repair bill eventually topped £55 million. The riots rapidly spread to other prisons and a public inquiry led by Lord Woolf recommended major reform to the prison service.

ABOVE: Richard Gere and Julia Roberts in a scene from the 1990 romantic comedy *Pretty Woman*. The film told the story of a wealthy businessman who hired a struggling prostitute. Directed by Garry Marshall and also starring Ralph Bellamy, the movie went on to achieve a BAFTA award for Best Film while Julia Roberts was nominated for an Academy Award for Best Actress. The soundtrack was highly successful with the song "Oh Pretty Woman" by Roy Orbison inspiring the film's title.

OPPOSITE: Princess Diana, accompanied by Princes William and Harry, visits the Portland Hospital, London, where Prince Andrew's wife Sarah had given birth to their second daughter, Princess Eugenie Victoria Helena.

A huge crowd gathers for Super Bowl XXV on January 27, 1991 in Tampa, Florida. The game was overshadowed by the First Gulf War, reflected in the highly patriotic pre-game ceremonies and entertainment that included an emotional rendering of "The Star-Spangled Banner" by Whitney Houston. The game is most remembered for the failed last-minute scoring attempt by Bills placekicker, Scott Norwood, which resulted in the New York Giants defeating the Buffalo Bills 20–9 and ushered in a run of Super Bowl disappointments for the Bills.

1991

Iraq invaded Kuwait in August 1990: the justification was an old territorial claim on the Gulf state but the main reasons were economic. Iraq had built enormous debts with its neighbors, Saudi Arabia and Kuwait, during the Iraq–Iran War and one solution was to annex oil-rich Kuwait. The Iraq invasion was swift and successful: Saddam Hussein appointed a cousin as governor and appeared on TV with Western hostages. Iraq could be forgiven for thinking they could act in their own back yard with impunity: they had been armed by US and Saudi Arabia in support of the war with Iran and were equipped for military victory. Following a UN resolution an international coalition force was assembled, led by the USA in Operation Desert Storm in January 1991.

After the support of overwhelming air superiority, US forces regained Kuwait City on February 23. As Iraqi troops withdrew they torched Kuwait's oil wells; the blazes took months to put out causing economic and environmental damage to the region. Many Iraqi troops quickly surrendered, while others formed a massive column retreating towards Baghdad. The column was bombed, killing hundreds, and more Iraqis were captured by advancing coalition forces. On February 28 President George Bush called a cease-fire, announcing the end of the First Gulf War.

1991

Abandoned vehicles line the "Highway of Death," the road between Kuwait City and Basra. Following the Allied invasion, Iraqi soldiers tried to flee Kuwait in any available means of transport, but most vehicles were intercepted and destroyed.

31

1991

ABOVE: His ill-considered and disastrous invasion of Kuwait did not shake Saddam Hussein personally, nor did it weaken his firm grasp of power in Iraq. The coalition cease-fire and apparent failure to optimize their strategic advantage puzzled many. The Bush administration recognized the cost of pursuing regime change; they also thought that Hussein would be overthrown by his own people after the defeat. Saddam would remain in power for another 12 years, allowing him to celebrate Bush's defeat in the 1993 election.

OPPOSITE: General H. Norman Schwarzkopf, also known as "Stormin' Norman," visits the Gulf War conflict zone. As coalition commander he directed Gulf War operations but he had measures and strategy in place with Operation Desert Shield well before Desert Storm was launched.

ABOVE: British Prime Minister, John Major, stands next to UK Gulf Forces Commander-in-Chief, Sir Peter de la Billiere during a visit to troops in the Arabian desert. They stand together on an impromptu podium formed by a tank. As second-in-command of the coalition forces, and with some knowledge of the area and local language, de la Billiere was able to advise coalition commander General Schwarzkopf on the use of special forces. De la Billiere had served with the SAS and was commander of the regiment during the London Iranian Embassy siege in 1980.

OPPOSITE: Chieftan tanks negotiate desert terrain during the war.

1991

ABOVE: Racing dynasties pose in the pits: from left to right, Wilson and Christian Fittipaldi, Derek and Justin Bell and Jackie and Paul Stewart. Damon Hill (far right), with support from Jackie Stewart, completes the quartet of young talent, three of whom were driving in the 1991 Formula 3000 season won by Christian Fittipaldi.

OPPOSITE: British Formula One Grand Prix winner, Nigel Mansell, waves to the crowd during his victory lap at Silverstone after stopping to give Ayrton Senna a lift back to the pits when the Brazilian was stranded on the track having run out of fuel.

The Marxist Derg regime, which had seized power in Ethiopia from Emperor Haile Selassie in 1974, was itself overthrown in 1991 when internal politics and a rebel coalition ended head of state Mengistu's disastrous rule. An estimated seven million people died in this period during which poverty and corruption became rife. While the task of government was not easy during the Derg period, Soviet backing gave them the upper hand against their opponents: the dissolution of the Soviet regime removed their advantage and they were supplanted by an interim coalition government until elections took place in 1995. Here government soldiers are held by victorious rebels after the fall of Addis Ababa in May 1991.

1991

GAY IS NO SHAME

GLAD TO BE GAY

RIGHT: Former Smiths' frontman Morrissey, performing at the Liverpool Empire. After major success with the Smiths throughout much of the 1980s, Morrissey embarked on a solo career late in the decade, and in 1991 he released his second solo album, *Kill Uncle*, written with Fairground Attraction's Mark E. Nevin, which peaked at number eight in the UK album charts. The supporting British tour introduced a new backing band lineup which was to prove a key ingredient for future success.

OPPOSITE: Jason Donovan is mobbed by gay rights campaigners as he leaves court, having begun legal proceedings against *The Face* magazine. In 1991, the publication printed doctored photographs of the singer and actor, which suggested that he was gay. That same year, Donovan accepted the lead role in Tim Rice and Andrew Lloyd Webber's *Joseph and the Amazing Technicolor Dreamcoat*, which provided him with his third UK number one single, "Any Dream Will Do."

1991

LEFT: In 1991, singer Whitney Houston was a massive star, scoring her ninth US number one single early in the year with the gospel-infused "All The Man That I Need," and performing "The Star-Spangled Banner" at Super Bowl XXV. The anthem was subsequently released as a single, with proceeds being donated to the Red Cross. Later in the year, Houston performed the *Welcome Home Heroes* concert for soldiers involved in the Gulf War, which drew record audiences when it was broadcast on HBO.

OPPOSITE: American rock star Bruce Springsteen, live onstage in 1992. Having dissolved the E Street Band in 1989, Springsteen set about working on new material, primarily with session musicians, and by late 1991 he had recorded two albums' worth of music, which would emerge as *Human Touch* and *Lucky Town* in 1992. Meanwhile, Springsteen was to marry his backing singer Patti Scialfa in June 1991, and six months later, she gave birth to their second child, Jessica Rae.

1991

ABOVE: Kevin Costner on the set of *Robin Hood: Prince of Thieves*. Earning $165 million in the United States and $225 million abroad, it was second only to *Terminator 2: Judgment Day* in worldwide ticket sales in 1991.

OPPOSITE: Opera star Luciano Pavarotti performs onstage at an outdoor concert in London's Hyde Park in 1991, drawing a record crowd of 150,000 fans, despite torrential rain. The previous year, Pavarotti found international fame, outside the world of classical music, with Puccini's "Nessun Dorma", which became one of the biggest-selling classical records of all time. Singing with Placido Domingo and Jose Carreras, the Three Tenors established a tradition of outdoor performance, returning the great tenor arias to popularity with a new young audience.

A cheering crowd of Ethiopian youths surrounds the toppled statue, sculptured in a pure style of socialist realism, of Russian Bolshevik revolutionary leader, Vladimir Ilyich Lenin on May 23, 1991 in Addis Ababa. Two days earlier, dictator Mengistu Haile Mariam fled to exile in Zimbabwe after being overthrown by the Ethiopian People's Democratic Front.

1991

OPPOSITE: Action by workers in Liverpool led to household waste piling up on the streets and parks, in scenes reminiscent of 1979's "Winter of Discontent." The Thatcherite principles governing Britain for 10 years had alienated large numbers of the working population and encouraged militant opposition in parts of the country; this took different forms, sometimes riots and unrest, or as in the case of Liverpool, calculated political action across a broad range of targets.

RIGHT: Model Paula Hamilton poses with elephants as part of her crusade for the welfare of the species. She founded Tusk Force in 1989, a charity dedicated to eradicating the ivory trade.

1991

RIGHT: In 1991 Chesney Hawkes shot to fame with the Nick Kershaw-penned single "The One and Only," which topped the UK chart for some five weeks and later reached the US top 10. The song was taken from the film *Buddy's Song*, which was released later in the year and starred Hawkes as the eponymous Buddy—a young man trying to make it as a pop star, under the guidance of his father, who was portrayed by The Who's Roger Daltrey.

OPPOSITE: Rolling Stones guitarist Keith Richards pictured performing on stage in Seville, Spain. Following the epic Steel Wheels/Urban Jungle tour, the Stones took a break from touring and recording, although they would release the live album *Flashpoint*, which included the studio track and single "Highwire." Meanwhile, 1991 would also see the release of Richards' own album, *Live at the Hollywood Palladium on December 15, 1988*, which was credited to Keith Richards and the X-Pensive Winos.

1991

ABOVE: England and Tottenham Hotspur midfielder Paul Gascoigne is stretchered from the pitch at Wembley during the 1991 FA Cup final against Nottingham Forest. Only minutes into the match, Gascoigne ruptured his right cruciate ligament as a result of a tackle against Forest defender Gary Charles. Tottenham went on to win the match 2–1 in extra time, but "Gazza" was unable to play again until late 1992.

OPPOSITE: US athlete Carl Lewis, pictured winning the 100 meters final at the Tokyo World Athletics Championships, with Britain's Linford Christie finishing fourth. Although 30 years of age, Lewis won the event in the record time of 9.86 seconds, and also helped the 4 x 100 meters relay team to a record breaking victory. In addition, Lewis made history by beating Bob Beamon's record in the long jump, although this was instantly eclipsed by fellow American Mike Powell, in one of sports most dramatic competitions.

1991

ABOVE: Croatia declared its independence from Yugoslavia in 1991. Yugoslavia resisted this with military force, supported by Serbs in the new Croatian territory who did not want to secede from Yugoslavia but then began to fight the new Croatia for a state territory of their own. The so-called "Homeland War" took between 10,000 and 20,000 lives and introduced the term "ethnic cleansing" into the language. The war ended in 1995.

OPPOSITE: Pro-government Kamajor militia on patrol near a diamond mine during the Sierra Leone Civil War. The aims of the rebel Revolutionary United Front may have been political but they focused on owning the lucrative diamond business of the country. Leader Foday Sankoh pursued a brutal campaign of terror between 1991 and 2002, killing opponents, mutilating prisoners, destroying villages, and arming children as soldiers.

1991

The Revolutionary United Front (RUF) began their terror in eastern Sierra Leone, the location of the diamond mines, which was also close to the border with Liberia, itself torn apart by tribal warfare and a channel for arms and drugs that supported the RUF. As well as controlling the mines, another goal for the rebels was to capture the capital, Freetown, on the west coast. In this picture a member of the RUF is being attacked by a mob of government-loyalists in Freetown—their weapons are sticks and stones but elsewhere could be machetes or AK-47s. The impact of such weaponry at close quarters and often on the civilian population was devastating.

LEFT: In 1991 Nick Faldo, pictured here in action during the Ryder Cup at Kiawah Island, South Carolina, was at the height of his game and regarded as the best golfer in the world, winning six major titles in the period from 1987 to 1996. He played his first Ryder Cup in 1987, at the age of 21, and went on to win more points in the competition than any other competitor to date.

OPPOSITE: England play Australia in the Rugby World Cup Final at Twickenham in 1991. The second ever series final was won by Australia 12 points to 6. This dramatic action shows Paul Ackford (left) about to catch the ball in a match that disappointed England's fans, who were surprised by a change of the tactics which had brought the England team to the final.

ABOVE: In June 1991 Boris Yeltsin was elected President of the Russian Republic, defeating Soviet President Michail Gorbachev's candidate for the post. The reforms presided over by Gorbachev (above right), as head of state of the Soviet Union, were opposed by the political establishment and they attempted to depose him in a coup in August. Gorbachev's weakened position and the ensuing mass secession of Soviet member states led to the dissolving of the Soviet Union and Gorbachev's resignation in December 1991. The optimism surrounding Yeltsin's early years as President of the newly formed Russian Federation was short-lived as corruption took hold in the chaos surrounding Yeltsin's rapidly liberalized and privatized economy.

OPPOSITE: Russian President Boris Yeltsin waves to an enthusiastic crowd from the balcony of the Russian Parliament on August 19. At least 50,000 Russians gathered in support of Yeltsin who presented himself as the people's savior in securing the Moscow White House against the coup plotters.

Carl Lewis in action at the Barcelona Olympics. Once again, Lewis came up against stiff competition from Mike Powell in the long jump, although on this occasion he would triumph, winning gold with a jump of 8.67 meters. He also anchored the 4 x 100 meter relay team to another record-breaking win, completing the final leg in under nine seconds. Four years later, the 35-year-old Lewis astounded the world with another long jump gold in Atlanta, and in 1999 the Olympic Committee would name him as one of the sportsmen of the century.

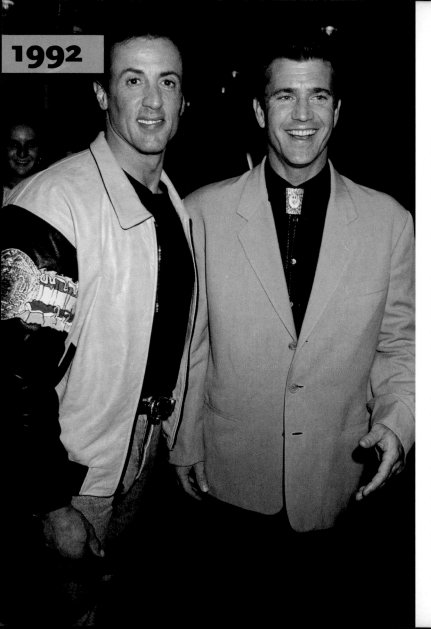

1992

LEFT: Sylvester Stallone with Mel Gibson. During the 1990s, Gibson used his box-office power to alternate between commercial and personal projects. His movies in the first half of the decade were *Forever Young*, *Lethal Weapon 3*, *Maverick*, and *Braveheart*.

OPPOSITE: Screen hard-men, Sylvester Stallone, Arnold Schwarzenegger, and Bruce Willis came together in 1992 to launch restaurant and movie shrine Planet Hollywood. Schwarzenegger's Harley-Davidson from the *Terminator* films was amongst the movie memorabilia on display. Willis's first role as a tough-guy came in 1988, playing John McLane in *Die Hard*, which spawned two successful sequels; *Die Hard 2* (1990), and *Die Hard: With a Vengeance* (1995). Action roles aside, Willis has gone on to show greater range and talent in such films as Quentin Tarantino's *Pulp Fiction* (1994) and *The Sixth Sense* (1999).

ABOVE: David Platt in action for England against Brazil at Wembley. In the Euro 92 tournament, England failed to win any of their group games and crashed out, with Platt scoring their only goal of the competition in a 2–1 defeat against Sweden.

OPPOSITE: Denzel Washington pictured in 1992, soon after he had completed filming the life story of the black activist *Malcom X*, directed by Spike Lee; this role would be the turning point of his career. The following year he consolidated his reputation as a courageous actor, playing a homophobic lawyer in the movie *Philadelphia*.

Former Prime Minister Margaret Thatcher stands at Victory Green, in the Falkland Islands' capital, Port Stanley, in June 1992 on the 10th anniversary of the end of the Falklands War. Her earlier visit seven months after the end of the war is celebrated each year as a public holiday in the Falklands: Margaret Thatcher Day, January 10.

1992

LEFT: Sean Penn at the Cannes film festival. While married to rock sensation Madonna, Penn established his reputation as an angry and volatile young man by assaulting a journalist in 1987, for which he received a short jail sentence. The incident did not adversely affect his reviews, or his reputation as a consistently good actor but confirmed him in a rebel role reminiscent of James Dean or Marlon Brando. The intensity he brought to many of his performances spilled over into his personal life as he became politically active.

OPPOSITE: Irish rock band U2 pictured recording the music video for their single, "Even Better Than The Real Thing," at the "ZOO" shop in London's Carnaby Street. The song was taken from the massively successful album *Achtung Baby*, which was supported by the extensive Zoo TV Tour. This employed some of the most elaborate staging ever attempted, with vast video walls, projectors, and television cameras being utilized to create a visually stunning multi-media spectacle.

LABOUR'S DOUBLE WHAMMY.

1. MORE TAXES

2. HIGHER PRICES

CONSERV

Despite Conservative Prime Minister John Major's dismantling of the highly unpopular "Poll Tax," with the 1992 general election looming, the UK had slipped into recession, and the Labour Party held the lead in the opinion polls. The Conservative's strategy was to focus on Labour's proposed spending plans, with the poster campaigns "Labour's Tax Bombshell" and "Labour's Double Whammy" proving particularly successful. But a headline on Election Day in the *Sun* newspaper, "If Kinnock wins today will the last person to leave Britain please turn out the lights," was widely blamed for the last-minute swing to the Conservatives.

In response to the Conservative Party's negative campaigning, the Labour Party quickly unveiled a budget, which detailed the party's tax and spending proposals, and attempted to rebut Conservative propaganda over hidden taxes. Labour claimed that 80 percent of voters would be better off under their plans, with the lowest earners benefiting the most. Pictured here is Labour's financial team: Shadow Chancellor John Smith (center), flanked by MPs Margaret Beckett and Chris Smith. Back row (L-R), Paul Boateng, Nick Brown, and Dr John Marek.

LEFT: Michael Jackson, live onstage in Bucharest during his Dangerous tour; the album it promoted proved to be one of his most successful, debuting at number one in both the US and UK in 1991, and spawning the massive hit singles "Black or White," "Remember the Time," "Jam," and "Heal the World." In 1992 Jackson established the Heal the World Foundation, which would raise millions of dollars to help underprivileged children around the world.

OPPOSITE: Michael Jackson pictured in London in 1992. Having set up his charitable foundation, Jackson announced that he would donate all profits from the Dangerous tour to the cause, before embarking on a highly publicized visit to Africa, where, in an Ivory Coast village, he was crowned "King Sani" by a tribal leader. Upon his return to the US, Jackson was awarded the title of "Living Legend" at the 35th Annual Grammy Awards.

1992

RIGHT: Radovan Karadzic, President of the newly formed Balkan state of Bosnia Herzegovina, arrives at the 1992 London Conference hosted by the EC to further a peace settlement in the Bosnian War. The first priority of the London Conference was to alleviate human suffering in the Bosnian conflict and specifically to stop all military flights over an agreed zone. In 1992 both Karadzic and Serbian President Slobodan Milosevic were concealing their true intentions via diplomacy and would be prosecuted for war crimes in the International Court of Justice.

OPPOSITE: British Chancellor, Norman Lamont, announces Britain's withdrawal from the Exchange Rate Mechanism (ERM) in September 1992. On September 16, a day now commonly referred to as "Black Wednesday," sterling dipped below the lower limit agreed in the terms of Britain's membership of the ERM and, unable to further prop up the value of sterling, Britain devalued it, after spending £27bn in reserves. Investor George Soros was blamed by some for instigating the crisis by short-selling $10bn in sterling, pocketing more than $1bn after the carnage was over.

1992

LEFT: Rock star Sting and actress Trudie Styler, pictured on their wedding day in 1992. The couple, who had been together for ten years, were married in a low-key ceremony in August, with just two close friends in attendance. That same year, Sting was awarded a Grammy for his single, "The Soul Cages," which won Best Rock Song; he also guest-starred in an episode of *The Simpsons*.

OPPOSITE: Throughout 1992 rock star Bryan Adams toured the globe, taking in Canada, Australia, New Zealand, and Europe. He also scored a major hit with the single "Thought I'd Died and Gone to Heaven," although its chart performance failed to come close to that of 1991's "(Everything I Do) I Do It for You," which had topped the charts in the UK, the US, Canada, and across much of Europe. As a result, the song won Best Song Written for a Motion Picture at the 1992 Grammy Awards.

1992

RIGHT: Despite her apparently happy countenance, by 1992 it was well known that Princess Diana's marriage was in trouble, due largely to the account given in Andrew Morton's book, *Diana: Her True Story*, which also contained revelations of the Princess's suicide attempts and struggle with an eating disorder. Before the end of the year, the separation of the royal couple would be formally announced.

OPPOSITE: Conservative Party leader John Major pictured on the campaign trail in his Huntingdon constituency, in the run-up to the April 1992 general election, where campaigning took a strange turn in both party camps. While John Major adopted an old fashioned style, speaking from an upturned soap-box, Neil Kinnock and his opposition team, with a clear lead in the polls, held an all-singing, all-dancing rally, in US presidential-style in a north of England arena the week before the election. Kinnock's excitable over-confidence struck the wrong note with the electorate and the Sheffield Rally, with a reputed cost of £100,000, is widely blamed for Labour's loss to the Conservatives by a margin of 8 percent of voting, in a massive electoral turn-out.

1992

The 1992 USA Men's Basketball Olympic Team pose for a team portrait in Barcelona, Spain: seated front row (L-R): Physician, Scottie Pippen, Christian Laettner, Patrick Ewing, Head Coach Chuck Daly, David Robinson, Karl Malone, Charles Barkley. Standing (L-R): Assistant coach Mike Krzyzewski, Assistant coach Lenny Wilkens, Michael Jordan, Larry Bird, Magic Johnson, Chris Mullin, Clyde Drexler, John Stockton, Assistant coach P.J. Carlesimo and trainer Ed LaCerte. Changes in regulations allowed professional players from the US NBA to participate for the first time in the 1992 Olympiad. The so-called "Dream Team" was one of the most illustrious the US has ever fielded for an international basketball competition.

1992

LEFT: Singer Tina Turner performing at the pre-opening gala for Disneyland Resort Paris, which opened its doors in 1992, despite controversy over the theme park's perceived negative impact on French culture. Turner, meanwhile, was enjoying a resurgence in popularity following her induction into the Rock and Roll Hall of Fame and the release of her compilation album *Simply the Best*, which included a newly recorded dance version of Turner's 1973 hit "Nutbush City Limits" amongst other rousing favorites.

OPPOSITE: Phil Collins, Mike Rutherford, and Tony Banks of the pop group Genesis, who enjoyed transatlantic chart success in 1992 with the singles "Hold On My Heart," "I Can't Dance," and "Jesus He Knows Me," as well as scoring a hit with the US-only release, "Never a Time." Four years later, Collins quit the band in order to focus on his solo career, although they would re-group in 1999 to record a new version of 1974's "The Carpet Crawlers."

1992

OPPOSITE: On June 25, 1992 a space shuttle was launched from Cape Canaveral in Florida, the twelfth mission of the *Columbia* orbiter. Crewed by five men and two women, the mission lasted just over 13 days and landed successfully on July 9. It was the longest space shuttle mission so far and carried the first United States Microgravity Laboratory into space to conduct experiments.

RIGHT: 1992 was the season that Formula One racer Nigel Mansell finally came good. It may have been due to his driving in the new Williams model, with its active suspension, but combined with Mansell's fierce determination to prove his critics wrong, the championship was achieved with nine victories that season.

OPPOSITE: Chelsea, Bill, and Hillary Clinton during the 1992 presidential campaign. In 1978 Clinton was elected Governor of Arkansas and became a leading figure among the New Democrats. After securing the Democratic party nomination he went on to win the Presidential election with 43 percent of the vote against Republican incumbent George Bush and billionaire independent Ross Perot. His win gave the Democrats full control of the United States Congress for the first time since the late 1970s.

ABOVE: Bill Clinton stretching after a jog at Louisiana State University.

1992

ABOVE: Prime Minister John Major greets Nelson Mandela at 10 Downing Street on February 7, 1992. On the same day Geoffrey Hurd, the British Foreign Secretary, was in the Netherlands signing the Maastricht Treaty. The treaty created the pillar structure of the European Union and the eventual euro currency.

OPPOSITE: Linford Christie clinches gold in the 100 meters at the 1992 Barcelona Olympic Games with a time of 9.96 seconds. At the age of 32 he became the oldest athlete to win this title.

1992

LEFT: David Bowie performing during the Freddie Mercury Tribute Concert for AIDS Awareness held at Wembley Stadium in April 1992. All 72,000 tickets sold out within four hours and the concert was televised and shown worldwide to an estimated audience of 1.2 billion. Brian May, John Deacon, and Roger Taylor, the three remaining members of Queen, performed with guests including Bowie, Elton John, George Michael, and Paul Young.

OPPOSITE: On the first anniversary of Freddie Mercury's death fans gathered outside his previous home at Garden Lodge in Kensington, where long-term friend Mary Austin continued to live. The Queen frontman contracted the HIV virus and eventually died due to AIDS-related bronchopneumonia. He was responsible for writing many of the band's hits including "Bohemian Rhapsody" and "Killer Queen."

1993

Greg Norman putts on the final green during the 1993 British Open at Royal St. George's Golf Club, as the capacity crowd holds its breath. Norman achieved the lowest closing round score by an Open winner in the 133-year history of the Championship, which was founded in 1860. Improvements made on his swing by working with instructor Butch Harmon were credited with Norman's return to top form in the mid 1990s.

122nd OPEN GOLF CHAMPIONSHIP · UNISYS

LEADER BOARD

HOLE	PAR	PLAYER	SCORE
71	-13	NORMAN	
71	-11	FALDO	
72	-10	LANGER	
70	9	PAVIN	
			POSITION AFTER 71 HOLES
72	8	SENIOR	272
72	6	ELS	274
72	6	LAWRIE	274
72	6	PRICE N.	275
72	5	GRADY	275
72	5	COUPLES	275
72	5	SIMPSON	275

PLAYER	
GAME NO 39	
FALDO	
PAVIN	
GAME NO 38	
LANGER	-10
NORMAN	-13

1993

OPPOSITE: Diana with her sons, Princes Harry and William, visit Thorpe Park near Windsor, taking full advantage of the rides but adhering to her policy that the boys should stand in line along with all the other children and did not receive special treatment. A major part of the Wales's separation negotiations had been over Charles and Diana's access to their sons in order to minimize the effect of the split.

ABOVE: Diana receives flowers from the crowd. In January 1993 yet another bombshell had been dropped—the full transcript of secretly recorded conversations between Charles and Camilla Parker Bowles was published in the national press.

1993

OPPOSITE: Hollywood stars Tom Cruise and Nicole Kidman in 1993. In 1990, the same year he and Kidman started their romance, Tom Cruise received a Best Actor Oscar nomination for his role as Vietnam veteran Ron Kovic in Oliver Stone's *Born on the Fourth of July*, following this success with excellent performances in *A Few Good Men* (1992), notable for its climactic courtroom scenes with Cruise and Jack Nicholson, and another legal thriller *The Firm* (1993).

RIGHT: Halle Berry first entered the limelight by winning several American beauty contests then moved into the world of modeling before gaining parts on TV's *Knots Landing* and *Living Dolls*. Her first film was Spike Lee's *Jungle Fever* in 1991, when she played the part of a crack addict. Berry reportedly took a method-actor approach, refusing to bathe for several days before filming, to enhance her performance.

1993

LEFT: *Superman* star Christopher Reeve with his wife Dana. In 1993 he starred in the period movie *Remains of the Day*. Better known in his role as the comic strip hero, Reeve was to become a real hero after a riding accident in 1995 left him paralysed from the neck down and unable to breath unaided. Determined to walk again, he became a campaigner for spinal injury research and managed to continue working from time to time before his tragic death on October 10, 2004.

OPPOSITE: After attending Yale Drama School, Sigourney Weaver landed the part of Warrant Officer Ripley in *Alien* in 1978; Weaver was not originally cast in that role but during filming Ridley Scott decided to make her the pivotal character. The part of Ripley was written so the role could be played by either gender. In 1993 she starred opposite Kevin Kline in White House comedy-drama *Dave*. Her portrayal of Dian Fossey in *Gorillas in the Mist* was a career high and encouraged her to become a high-profile conservationist.

ABOVE: A production still from Steven Spielberg's 1993 drama *Schindler's List*, which tells the true story of German businessman Oskar Schindler, who saved hundreds of Polish Jews from death by employing them as skilled factory workers. Spielberg had first been approached to make the movie ten years earlier, but at that time had reservations about his ability to do justice to the subject matter. The film won Spielberg critical acclaim around the world and received seven Academy Awards.

OPPOSITE: In 1993 Roy Keane was enjoying his first season with Manchester United after his transfer from struggling Nottingham Forest for a record fee of £3.75 million. Viewed as the hottest young player around, he was in the middle of a deal with Kenny Dalglish to join Blackburn Rovers when Alex Ferguson stepped in with his offer. Here, playing for his national team, the Republic of Ireland, Keane tackles Holland's Marc Overmars.

1993

Running back Lincoln Coleman, number 44 of the Dallas Cowboys, is wrapped up by the Miami Dolphins' defence at Texas Stadium on November 25, 1993 in Irving, Texas. A freak snow and sleet storm in Dallas set the stage for a wild finish as the Dolphins attempted a field goal to put them on top with a few seconds left in the game. The Cowboys blocked the kick and, while most of the team celebrated what should have been an automatic victory, DT Leon Lett attempted to recover the ball. Instead, he slipped on the ice and kicked the ball further into Dallas territory. Miami recovered the ball on the Dallas one-yard line. Pete Stoyanovich nailed the second field goal attempt and the Dolphins won 16–14. Dallas beat the Bills in the Superbowl earlier that year and Miami should not have been an obstacle. In the words of a commentator, "Lett's blunder will live on as one of the all-time greatest bonehead plays in professional sports."

1993

LEFT: The Palestinian leader Yasser Arafat arrives in London. This was Arafat's first visit to Britain, during which he participated in important discussions over the future of the Middle East peace process. Earlier in the year, he had attended the historic Oslo Accords, which marked the first successful face-to-face negotiations between Israeli and Palestinian leaders. As a result, Arafat, Israel's Prime Minister Yitzhak Rabin, and Foreign Minister Shimon Peres would share the Nobel Peace Prize in 1994.

OPPOSITE: Singer Alison Moyet pictured performing live at Glastonbury in 1993. Other artists appearing at the festival that year included Robert Plant, Lenny Kravitz, The Orb, and Rolf Harris. The following year, Moyet issued her fourth studio album, *Essex*, and in 1995 her record label, Sony, released the chart-topping greatest hits package, *Singles*. However, by this time Moyet was seeking a release from her recording contract, which Sony resisted until 2002 and during this period her recording activity was limited to backing vocals.

1993

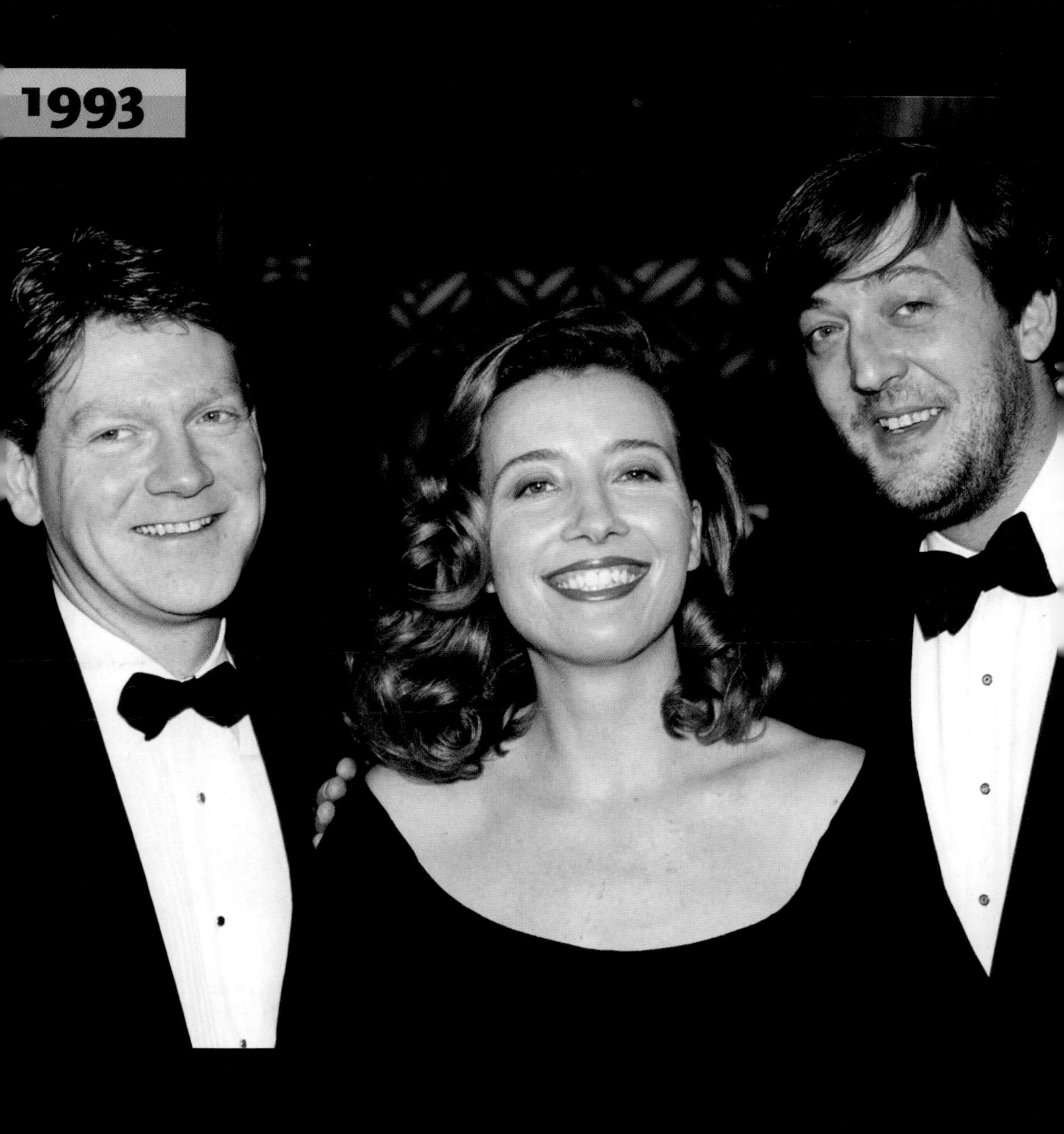

RIGHT: Pop star George Michael arriving at the High Court in London, having launched legal proceedings against his record label, Sony. The singer was attempting to extricate himself from his contract with the company due to grievances over their failure to adequately promote his album *Listen Without Prejudice Vol. 1*, as well as perceived restrictions on his artistic freedom. Sony would ultimately win the case in July 1994, although they agreed to release Michael from his contract the following year.

OPPOSITE: Kenneth Branagh, Emma Thompson, and Stephen Fry. In 1992 Thompson was recognized for her performances in both Branagh's *Much Ado About Nothing* and *Remains of the Day*. In 1993 she and Branagh were still married and the two were regarded as a golden showbiz couple. Thompson and Fry were Cambridge Footlights colleagues and renewed their acting partnership in the 1992 movie *Peter's Friends*, which was also directed by Branagh.

LEFT: Madonna on stage during The Girlie Show world tour in September 1993, in support of her *Erotica* album. Madonna starred in two 1993 movies, *Body of Evidence* and *Dangerous Game*, the latter being the first production of Madonna's own Maverick Picture Company. At this point in her career Madonna was recklessly using her sexuality in her artistic career, with her explicit book *Sex* as a starting point. Audience reactions persuaded her to tone down her act after the Girlie Show tour.

OPPOSITE: Israeli troops respond to a group of Palestinian stone-throwers in the Jebaliya refugee camp in the Gaza Strip. It was here that the 1987 Intifada first began in response to the deaths of four Palestinians blamed on Israeli forces.

1993

ABOVE: A scene from Steven Spielberg's *Jurassic Park*, featuring Jeff Goldblum, Sir Richard Attenborough, Laura Dern, and Sam Neill. Based on Michael Crichton's science fiction novel of the same name, the movie enjoyed worldwide takings of over $914 million, to become the highest-grossing film of all time, a record that would stand until the release of James Cameron's *Titanic* five years later.

OPPOSITE: Flamboyant rock star Elton John wraps up a call in his limousine after the courts awarded him £350,000 libel damages against the *Daily Mirror*, which ran a fictitious story about an eating disorder.

112

1993

LEFT: German tennis star Steffi Graf, pictured after winning her first-round match at Wimbledon. In 1993, Graf re-established her dominance of the women's singles game by winning the French and US Open tournaments for the third time, and by scoring her fifth victory at Wimbledon. However, earlier in the year she had been defeated by Monica Seles in the final of the Australian Open, prompting a deranged fan to stab Seles during a match in Hamburg, Germany.

OPPOSITE: Manager of the England soccer team, Graham Taylor, calls from the touchline in Rotterdam, where his side were facing the Netherlands in a desperate bid to qualify for the 1994 World Cup. The second half began level at 0–0, but goals from Ronald Koeman and Dennis Bergkamp put the game beyond England's grasp. A few weeks later, England would beat San Marino 7–0, but the Netherlands' victory over Poland on the same night put England out of the competition, and Taylor resigned within days.

1993

Joe Carter, number 29 of the Toronto Blue Jays, hits a game winning three-run home run against the Philadelphia Phillies in game six of the 1993 World Series at SkyDome on October 23, 1993. The Blue Jays defeated the Phillies 8-6, winning the World Series for the second season in a row. To date the Blue Jays are the only non–US team to have won the World Series.

1993

LEFT: Swedish-born television presenter Ulrika Jonsson made her name as a weather girl for TV-am before she began presenting the *Gladiators* game show in 1992. She continued to front the show throughout the 1990s as well as appearing in BBC 2's comedy quiz show, *Shooting Stars*, as a team captain. Jonsson's colorful personal life gave her a high profile in the tabloid press which continues today thanks in part to her participation in the likes of *Celebrity Big Brother*, which she won in 2009.

OPPOSITE: Having been used to bear the burden of the world's problems it's a big change to just worry about his own baggage! Former US President George Bush flies in to London with wife Barbara. His low-key arrival was a far cry from the VIP treatment he received when he was the most powerful man on the planet.

1993

ABOVE: Photographed by his wife Linda, former Beatle Paul McCartney and their Old English Sheepdog walk across Abbey Road on the famous zebra crossing that provided the iconic cover of the Beatles 1969 *Abbey Road* LP. The occasion was a photoshoot for McCartney's *Paul is Live* album released toward the end of 1993, having launched his first album of the 1990s, *Off the Ground*, earlier in the year.

OPPOSITE: Bob Dylan arrives in London for another leg of his Never Ending Tour that kicked off in 1988. While in London, Dylan shot footage for the *Blood in My Eyes* video in black and white with handheld cameras. Earlier in the year he performed "Chimes of Freedom" at President Bill Clinton's inauguration ceremonies.

1993

ABOVE: Following on from her 1990 work, *Ghost*, which first brought her to the attention of the public, in 1993 sculptor Rachel Whiteread became the first female winner of the £20,000 Turner Prize, which was awarded for her work *House*— a concrete cast of the interior of a Victorian house situated on Grove Road in East London. She also received Bill Drummond and Jimmy Cauty's £40,000 K Foundation award for "Worst Artist of the Year." *House* is pictured here being demolished by Tower Hamlets council in early 1994.

OPPOSITE: Roman Catholic nun and art critic, Sister Wendy Beckett, pictured at the Royal Academy's Summer Exhibition in London. During the 1990s, Sister Wendy found fame with a series of books and television documentaries on the history of art, including *Sister Wendy's Odyssey, Sister Wendy's Grand Tour,* and *Sister Wendy's Story of Painting*. More recently, her life story inspired the stage production, *Postcards from God: Sister Wendy The Musical*.

ABOVE AND OPPOSITE: Tourists line up in their thousands to visit Buckingham Palace. In 1993 the decision was made to allow visitors to tour the Queen's London residence during the months of August and September while the Royal Family was at Balmoral. Visits were priced at £8 per adult and profits were used to pay for 70 percent of the £40 million needed to restore Windsor Castle after a devastating fire the previous year. 380,000 people visited in the first summer and were able to view the State apartments, including the East Gallery (pictured) hung with priceless paintings from the Royal Collection. Visitors could also experience the view from the famous balcony.

1993

On September 13, 1993, Palestine Liberation Organization leader Yasser Arafat shakes hands with Israeli Prime Minister Yitzhak Rabin on the White House lawn as President Bill Clinton looks on. Rabin, Arafat, and Israel's Foreign Minister, Shimon Peres came together in Washington DC to sign the first Israel-PLO framework for autonomy in West Bank, Gaza, the most tangible step to date in the Middle East Peace Process which would pave the way for an elected government for the Palestinian people.

1994

The 1994 San Marino Grand Prix at Imola, Italy, was a race marred by tragedy after the death of two racing drivers in as many days. Thirty-one-year-old Austrian novice driver Roland Ratzenberger was killed in a high-speed crash during a qualifying session. This tragedy was compounded the next day when the Brazilian Formula One World Champion Ayrton Senna died during the race when his Williams car spun off the track at the Tamburello curve and smashed into a concrete wall. Senna—considered one of the finest Formula One drivers of his generation—was mourned by racing fans around the world.

1994

RIGHT: Considered to be one of the best actors of his generation, Robert De Niro has played a wealth of characters with both charisma and formidable authority, establishing his style in Martin Scorsese's *Mean Streets* in 1973 and continuing to receive accolades for the rest of his career. In the early 1990s he was nominated by the Academy for Best Actor for both *Cape Fear* and *Awakenings* (1991). De Niro has his own production company called Tribeca Film Center and made his directorial debut in 1993 with *A Bronx Tale*. He is pictured at the British Film Awards in 1994.

OPPOSITE: In 1994, Tom Hanks won Best Actor for his portrayal of an AIDS sufferer in *Philadelphia*, and went on to win the award the following year for *Forrest Gump*, the first actor to win in successive years since Spencer Tracy in 1937 and 1938.

1994

American figure-skaters Nancy Kerrigan and Tonya Harding ignore each other during a practise session at the Lillehammer Winter Olympics. In the previous month Olympic favorite Kerrigan had been attacked as she left the ice after a practise session during the Figure Skating Championships in Detroit. It later transpired that Harding's ex-husband, Jeff Gillooly, had hired an accomplice to assault Kerrigan in order to force her to withdraw from competition. However, Kerrigan recovered in time to compete in Lillehammer where she finished in second place behind the Ukrainian World Champion Oksana Baiul, while Harding finished in eighth place.

1994

ABOVE: Bruce Willis makes a guest appearance behind the bar at Planet Hollywood He was well qualified for the job, having worked as a bar-tender before his big break in acting.

OPPOSITE: Johnny Depp with girlfriend and model Kate Moss in 1994. Between 1993 and 1994 Depp was to make no less than four movies: *Benny & Joon*, *What's Eating Gilbert Grape*, *Ed Wood* and *Arizona Dream*.

ABOVE AND OPPOSITE: In August 1992 Fred West was arrested for raping his daughter; during the court case police were given a lead, which, in 1994, took them to the "house of horror"—the West home in Gloucester—where they excavated the interior and the gardens. Among the nine bodies that were exhumed was that of Fred and Rosemary West's daughter, Heather, who vanished when she was 16. It was a "family joke" that if the other children did not behave, they would end up under the patio like Heather. The web of sexual abuse and violent crime uncovered in the case astonished the British people. West, jailed for 12 murders, hanged himself in prison the following year; for her part in the crimes his wife was sentenced to spend the rest of her life behind bars. In 1996 the Cromwell Street house was completely destroyed and the rubble was pulverized to prevent souvenir hunting.

1994

RIGHT: In a stunning off-the-shoulder cocktail dress designed by Christina Stambolian, Diana, Princess of Wales attended the *Vanity Fair* party at the Serpentine gallery. On the same evening a documentary about Prince Charles: *Charles: The Private Man, the Public Role*, was screened on British television. Broadcaster Jonathan Dimbleby and a television crew had followed the Prince for 18 months and during the interview Charles admitted to adultery after his marriage to Diana had broken down. The following day in a press conference, the Prince's private secretary Richard Aylward named Camilla Parker Bowles as the other woman in his life.

OPPOSITE: Elizabeth Hurley and boyfriend Hugh Grant arrive for the premiere of the romantic comedy, *Four Weddings and a Funeral*, in which Grant starred. The film went on to gross over $244 million worldwide, making it the most financially successful British movie at that time, whilst Hurley's profile was massively boosted by the Versace "safety-pin" dress that she appeared in on the red carpet. In 1994, the couple also founded Simian Films, which would go on to make *Extreme Measures* and *Mickey Blue Eyes*.

1994

Bosnian Serb soldiers cover their ears as they fire a missile at Bosnian Muslim positions in the city of Bihac. The Bihac pocket was besieged for nearly three years and at one point in 1994 40,000 Muslim refugees were expelled by forces under General Dudakovic into the neighboring region known as the Krajina. The Bosnian War had a bewildering number of belligerent parties. A ceasefire between two of them resulted in the establishing of the Federation of Bosnia-Herzegovina which today is a territory of the State of Bosnia-Herzegovina. The remaining warring parties continued through 1995 in a period of unprecedented bloodletting that ended with the Daytona Peace Agreement in December.

During the Bosnian War the UN Protection Force often had its hands tied because of strict rules of engagement, powerlessly observing humanitarian crimes. It was common for neutral UN personnel to be fired on by any of the belligerent parties. In this picture a UN helicopter patrol monitors the frontline near Sarajevo Airport after reports that UN planes were coming under sniper fire. However, in 1994 NATO intervened to enforce the no-fly zone in Bosnian air space.

1994

RIGHT: Pop singer Bob Geldof pictured with his wife Paula Yates. Having previously presented quirky TV music show, *The Tube*, alongside Jools Holland, Yates became a regular on Channel 4's morning show, *The Big Breakfast*, made by Geldof's Planet 24 production company. Amongst the guests interviewed "in bed" with Yates in 1994 was INXS frontman Michael Hutchence, and by the following year, the pair had embarked upon a well-publicized affair, with the result that she and Geldof were divorced in 1996. Yates's relationship with Hutchence would end in tragedy.

OPPOSITE: Irish boyband, Boyzone, was put together in 1993 by music industry manager and talent judge, Louis Walsh. Before even recording any material they made a now infamous appearance on RTÉ's *The Late Late Show*. Their first album *Said and Done* was released in 1995. (L-R) Stephen Gately, Mikey Graham, Shane Lynch, Keith Duffy, and Ronan Keating.

1994

OPPOSITE: In 1990 Tutsi people who had fled Rwanda in the late 1950s crossed the border from Uganda into northern Rwanda under the Rwandan Popular Front political banner, creating serious tensions with their arch-enemy the Hutu people, who held political dominance in Rwanda. Violence erupted in 1994 when a plane carrying the presidents of both Rwanda and Burundi was shot down, killing them both. Here the bodies of Tutsi victims lie outside a church in Rukura where more than 4,000 people were killed while taking refuge. Mass murders in churches and schools were a recurring feature of the genocide.

ABOVE: The Hutus had the upper hand at the start of the conflict in Rwanda; however, the Tutsis proved the victors, though suffering the same horrors they meted out to their opponents. Both sides in the conflict massacred innocent civilians including children; rape and mutilation were the rule. In this picture, some of the hundreds of thousands of Hutu refugees pour over the Tanzanian border to escape the RPF onslaught in May 1994.

1994

ABOVE: Flamboyant British film director and producer, Ken Russell, pictured at his London home in 1994. Although best known for the Oscar-winning *Women in Love*, and more contentious movies such as *The Devils* and *Whore*, during the early 1990s Russell also became known as a writer of film criticism. In 1993 he published *Fire Over England: British Cinema Comes Under Friendly Fire*, which was followed by *The Lion Roars: Ken Russell on Film* in 1994.

OPPOSITE: The Chancellor of the Exchequer, Kenneth Clarke, pictured with his wife Gillian, in the luxurious surroundings of their ministerial retreat, Dorneywood. In the aftermath of "Black Wednesday", Norman Lamont's position had become increasingly untenable, and so in May 1993, he was succeeded as Chancellor by Clarke. By the following year, the new Chancellor had already established himself as a powerful figure within the Conservative Cabinet, and in his 1994 budget he would announce the biggest public spending cuts in a decade.

1994

A dramatic scene from the 1994 Grand National at Aintree Race Course, Merseyside. The previous year, the race ended in chaos and had to be declared void after two false starts, but there were no such problems in 1994, and jockey Richard Dunwoody secured the second Grand National win of his career, on this occasion riding Miinnehoma, a horse owned by British comedian Freddie Starr. Dunwoody was also awarded a third consecutive Lester Award for "Best Jump Jockey of the Year".

ABOVE: Two policemen monitor a curfew in Colombo, capital of Sri Lanka, following a bomb blast in October 1994; a virtual war was waged between the Sinhalese majority and the Tamil minority from 1983. The so-called Tamil Tigers adopted terror tactics both in Sri Lanka and in India, killing former Indian Prime Minister Rajiv Gandhi in 1991 and then Sri Lankan President Premadasa in 1993 with suicide bombings. After a bitter struggle the Tigers were declared eliminated in 2009.

OPPOSITE: In 1994 Queen Elizabeth and Prince Philip made a historic state visit to Russia, where they met with President Boris Yeltsin, his wife Naina, and the Mayor of Moscow, Yuri Luzhkov. The group toured the Kremlin and Red Square, with the Queen laying a wreath at the Tomb of the Unknown Soldier in the Alexander Garden beside the Kremlin Wall.

1994

ABOVE: Actress Joanna Lumley pictured at a demonstration against live animal exports. During the early 1990s, Lumley's career was enjoying something of a resurgence on account of her role as Patsy in the BBC comedy, *Absolutely Fabulous*, but she also found fame as an outspoken campaigner, notably as a patron of "Compassion In World Farming", and in 1994 Lumley helped to produce the documentary For a Few Pennies More, which highlighted the terrible conditions and treatment endured by animals being exported for slaughter.

OPPOSITE: The Edge, guitar anchor of rock band U2, pictured at the 39th Annual Ivor Novello Awards ceremony. In 1994, U2 won an Ivor Novello for International Achievement, a Grammy Award for Best Alternative Music Performance, a World Music Award for Best Selling Irish Recording Artist of the Year and a *Q* magazine Merit Award. In addition, the band was also nominated for an American Music Award in the category of Favorite Pop / Rock Group.

Labour

Leadership
challenge

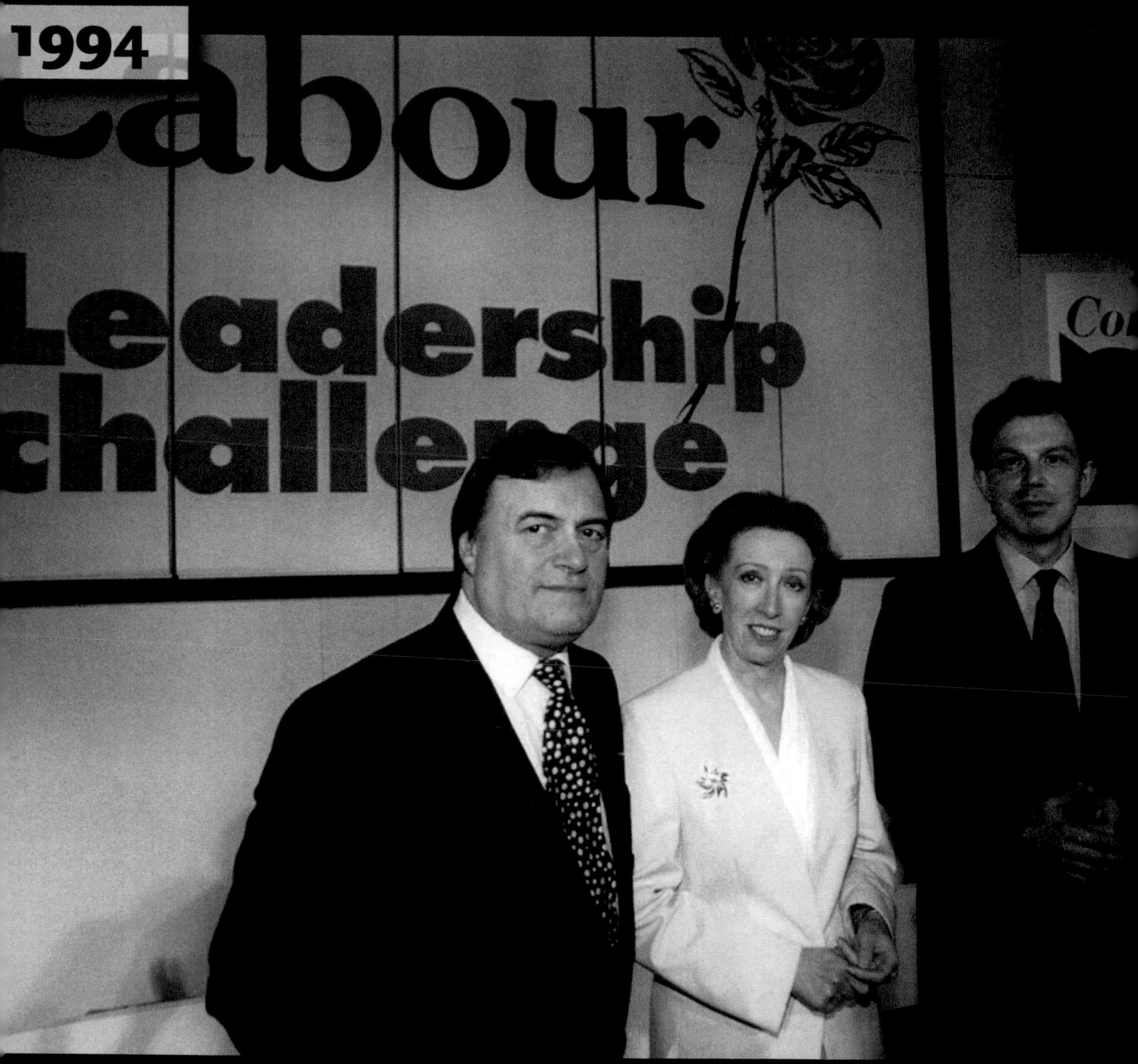

OPPOSITE: In July, two months after the sudden death of the Labour leader John Smith, the party held a leadership election, with acting leader Margaret Beckett, John Prescott, and Tony Blair standing as candidates. The election was the first of its kind since the introduction of "One Member One Vote" the previous year, a system that had been championed by Prescott. Ultimately however, it was Blair that would emerge victorious, with Prescott going on to win the subsequent vote for the position of deputy leader.

RIGHT: Antony Gormley's sculptural installation, *Testing a World View*, on show at London's Tate Gallery. Along with *Field for the British Isles*, which consisted of around 40,000 small terracotta figures arranged to fill the floor-space of a room, the artwork formed part of Gormley's Turner Prize-winning exhibition in 1994.

1994

ABOVE: A Eurostar train at the new international rail terminal at Waterloo Railway Station. On November 14, 1994 Eurostar services began between Waterloo International in London, Gare du Nord in Paris, France, and Brussels-South railway station in Belgium, the trains traveling through an under-sea tunnel which links England with France.

OPPOSITE: US soul singer Luther Vandross pictured outside the Royal Albert Hall in Kensington, West London, where he was performing for a US television special, which would later be released on DVD as *Luther Vandross—Always and Forever*. Soon after the concert, Vandross released his ninth studio album, Songs, which included the hit singles "Ain't No Stoppin' Us Now" and "Endless Love," which featured Mariah Carey. The album went on to earn four Grammy Award nominations.

1994

Racing driver Michael Schumacher pictured in 1994, the year he won the Formula One Drivers' Championship for the first time. Driving for Benetton he won six of the season's first seven races. However, during a very eventful year Schumacher was disqualified for technical issues from the British and Belgian Grand Prix and at the start of the final race in Australia was in the lead but only one point clear of Damon Hill. During the race Schumacher clipped the wall and steered into the path of Hill forcing them both to retire. This resulted in Schumacher winning the Championship, albeit in controversial circumstances, as many believed he had deliberately caused the collision.

ABOVE: Chairman of the PLO and President of the Palestinian National Authority, Yasser Arafat, Foreign Minister of Israel, Shimon Perez and Prime Minister of Israel, Yitzakh Rabin, share the 1994 Nobel Peace Prize for their efforts to create peace in the Middle East. The ceremony in Oslo caused controversy and was marred by the resignation of Kaare Kristiansen from the Nobel committee by way of protest. For his role in the Oslo Accords Rabin would be assassinated the following year by one of his own people.

OPPOSITE: Rwandan refugees stand beside dead bodies awaiting burial after fleeing their country during the Rwandan Civil War. In the aftermath of the genocide an estimated 2 million Hutus fled to neighboring states, mainly Zaire, for refuge from Tutsi reprisals. Many thousands died in refugee camps from cholera and dysentery.

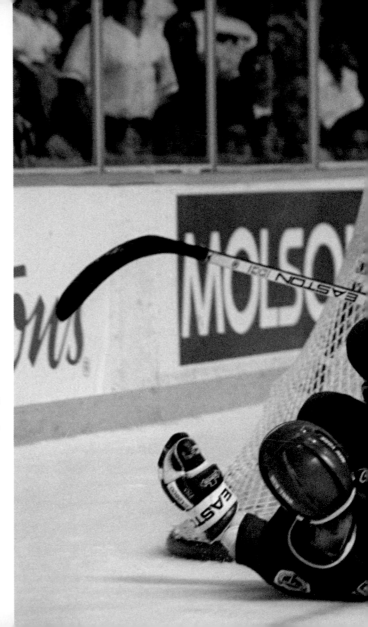

Alexei Kovalev of the New York Rangers scores a goal during the Stanley Cup Finals series against the Vancouver Canucks at the Pacific Coliseum in Vancouver, Canada. The Canucks were making the club's second appearance in a final, their first was during their Cinderella run of 1982. 1994 was the Rangers tenth final but their first since 1979. The Rangers ended their record 54 years without a championship win with a victory in Game 7 and claimed the cup in front of a rapturous home crowd at Madison Square Garden, New York City.

1994

ABOVE: Fan of the guitar from an early age, Damon Hill began a tradition of playing a gig after Grand Prix races with a collection of drivers and Formula One people, from Eddie Jordan on drums to David Coulthard seen here with maracas. Not that Hill needed an extra string to his bow during the 1994 season, which he lost by a single point to Michael Schumacher after a controversial crash caused by the German during the November Australian Grand Prix.

OPPOSITE: The Brazilian football team ready for their first round match against Cameroon in the 1994 World Cup held in the United States. Brazil were soon storming their way through the tournament and finally met Italy in a nail-biting final that went to overtime and then to penalties. Brazil emerged the victors beating the Italians 3-2, entering into the record books as the only team to win the World Cup four times.

1994

Millvina Dean and Edith
Haisman, the oldest and
youngest survivors of the
Titanic disaster visit an
exhibition of the ship's
artifacts in 1994. In 1985
the ship's wreck had been
discovered 370 miles south-
east of Newfoundland and
after several court cases
RMS Titanic Inc. was
granted ownership and
salvaging rights. In 1994 the
salvaging operation began
and around 6,000 artifacts
were successfully brought to
the surface, many of which
were exhibited at London's
National Maritime Museum
in Greenwich.

1995

LEFT: Europe celebrates a dramatic win over the United States in the 1995 Ryder Cup at Oak Hill Country Club, New York. The European team won the competition by a margin of 14½ to 13½ points to win back the Cup. The tournament was blessed with some dazzling golf, including two hole-in-ones from European golfers Howard Clarke and Costantino Rocca, and concluded in a nerve-jangling finish when the Europeans snatched a dramatic victory in the final holes.

ABOVE: Bernhard Langer and Ian Woosnam line up a putt during the 1995 Ryder Cup. The Europeans were captained for the third time by Bernard Gallacher while Lanny Wadkins took over as captain of the American team.

1995

LEFT: Scenes of destruction in Oklahoma City after a car bomb exploded at the Alfred P. Murrah federal government building in April. The bombing was timed to coincide with the second anniversary of the Waco Siege. The final death toll was 168 including 19 children, with nearly 700 injured. The home-made bomb in a rented truck was planted by American militia movement sympathizers Timothy McVeigh and Terry Nichols. McVeigh was executed with a lethal injection in 2001 while Nichols received a life sentence. Afterwards the American government passed new legislation to improve security and protection around federal buildings to prevent further attacks.

OPPOSITE: Tom Cruise greets fans at the premiere of *Interview with the Vampire* in which he starred as Lestat de Lioncourt. Cruise has been known to spend over an hour on the red carpet at such occasions, chatting, signing autographs and on one well publicized occasion, phoning a fan's mother, who was too busy to take the call. The adaptation of Anne Rice's bestselling novel is considerd to be one of the most intelligent horror films ever made.

ABOVE: The funeral of Ronnie Kray, March 17, 1995. The East End gangland twins Kray, Ronald and Reginald, were sentenced to life imprisonment on March 6, 1969, Mr Justice Melford Stevenson recommending that they should be detained for a minimum of 30 years—the longest sentences ever passed at the Central Criminal Court for murder.

OPPOSITE: Charlie and Reggie share a quiet moment at the graveside of brother Ronnie as he was buried with all the pomp and sentiment only London's East End can muster. Reggie was released from prison on compassionate grounds in August 2000, a few weeks before his death from cancer.

1995

The widely publicized O. J. Simpson trial concluded on October 3, 1995. The former NFL star and actor was on trial for the murder, in June 1994, of his estranged wife Nicole and her friend Ronald Goldman. When Simpson notoriously fled from arresting officers in a televised car chase many assumed him to be guilty. However, after only three hours of deliberation, the jury returned a verdict of not guilty for the two murders. The verdict was seen live on TV by more than half of the US population, making it one of the most watched events in American TV history.

1995

Edgar Martinez of the Seattle Mariners hits a three-run home run in the third inning of game four of the 1995 American League Divisional Series against the New York Yankees at the Kingdome, Seattle, Washington, on October 7, 1995. The Mariners defeated the Yankees 11–8 on their way to winning the series.

1995

RIGHT: Child soldiers man a checkpoint 60 miles outside the capital city, Freetown, in the Sierra Leone Civil War. The war erupted in 1991 amidst concerns about government corruption, mismanagement of the country's abundant diamond resources and arms trafficking and was notably characterized by the forced recruitment of child soldiers by rebel troops.

OPPOSITE: A heavily armed militiaman controls traffic on the streets of Freetown, Sierra Leone, during the country's decade-long Civil War. By 1995 the Revolutionary United Front (RUF) had taken control of the diamond-producing eastern region and had reached the outskirts of Freetown. A coup in 1992 had ousted President Momoh and installed the National Provisional Ruling Council in government. They employed foreign mercenaries to drive the RUF to the edge of Sierra Leone's borders but the war would continue for another seven years.

LEFT: President Bill Clinton had long called upon the international community to do more to assist the Bosnian Muslims, but other countries were worried that sending in more weapons and conducting airstrikes would jeopardize the safety of UN peacekeepers. In the event, several hundred peacekeepers were used as human shields by the Bosnian Serbs during Operation Deliberate Force.

OPPOSITE: Having pledged to send a peace envoy to Northern Ireland during his presidential campaign in 1992, on November 30, 1995, Bill Clinton became the first serving US president to visit the country. The previous year he had angered some by permitting Sinn Féin leader Gerry Adams to visit the US, but Clinton believed that peace could only be achieved by inclusive policies. He was greeted by thousands of people in Belfast, including Adams, with whom he famously shook hands on the Falls Road.

Anfernee Hardaway of
the Orlando Magic drives
to the basket against Jud
Buechler of the Chicago
Bulls in game six of
the Eastern Conference
Semi-finals during the
1995 NBA Playoffs at the
United Center in Chicago,
Illinois, on May 18. The
Orlando Magic defeated
the Chicago Bulls 108–102
and won the series
4–2, making it to the NBA
finals, to be defeated by
the Houston Rockets. The
newly formed franchise
were in their fourth
season, rising rapidly in
the NBA thanks to the
partnership of Shaquille
O'Neal, enrolled in the
1992 draft and "Penny"
Hardaway in the 1993
draft, immediately giving
the Magic a 50-win season
in 1993–94—a franchise
record.

ABOVE: American boy band, New Kids on the Block, were put together in Boston by producer Maurice Starr and gained a massive following as champions of Teen Rock in the late 1980s and early 1990s. Brothers Jordan and Jonathan Knight, Joey McIntyre, Donnie Wahlberg, and Danny Wood became the first American group to achieve six Top 5 hits in a row in the UK and won two American Music Awards in 1990. By 1994 their popularity had waned, their fourth album failed and in 1995 it was all over.

OPPOSITE: Legendary guitarist Mark Knopfler formed the hugely successful Dire Straits with younger brother David, John Illsley and Pick Withers in 1977 and was the driving force behind the group throughout the band's career. Dire Straits disbanded in 1988 to reform in 1991 with a different lineup, only to disband again in 1995; Knopfler continued to record and produce successful solo albums after the breakup.

1995

LEFT: In 1995 Irish actor Pierce Brosnan made his debut as James Bond in *GoldenEye*. He had been offered the role many years earlier but had to turn it down due to work commitments—his starring role in TV series *Remington Steele*. With the new Bond came a new M—Judy Dench, playing Bond's boss, perhaps inspired by the 1992 appointment of a woman to head UK's MI5. Brosnan went on to portray 007 in three more Bond films.

OPPOSITE: Buzz Lightyear, one of the main characters in *Toy Story*, the first full-length animated production from Pixar Studios, owned by Apple co-founder Steve Jobs from 1986. Lightyear's catchphrase "To infinity ... and beyond!" seemed to sum up the innovative movie, with its breathtaking computer-generated artistry. The movie was a massive box-office and commercial success, becoming a children's classic on DVD and generating huge merchandizing revenues.

Alex Ferguson

ABOVE: London-based Kiwis perform the traditional Maori haka in Covent Garden Piazza, in celebration of New Zealand's 45–29 victory over England in the 1995 Rugby World Cup semi-finals. The host nation, South Africa went on to win the competition, beating the All Blacks 15 points to 12. Following the final game, President Nelson Mandela presented the William Webb Ellis Cup to South Africa's captain Francois Pienaar, while sporting a Springboks rugby jersey and cap. The move was heralded as a further step towards national unity.

OPPOSITE: Alex Ferguson launches his autobiography at a press conference held at Old Trafford in July 1995. Glaswegian-born Ferguson came to Manchester United in November 1986, taking over from Ron Atkinson. He appointed Archie Knox as his assistant and immediately set to work to improve the players' discipline. Through new signings he steadily improved the team's performance and in 1990 they won the FA Cup. United clinched the League Cup the following year but had to wait until 1993 to win the prestigious Premier League title. 1994 saw the team win the League and Cup double with striker Eric Cantona scoring 25 goals.

1995

OPPOSITE: Initially signed to Warner Bros., George Clooney played several small supporting roles before coming to the public eye in the 1990s in the highly successful television series *ER*, which achieved number one ranking in the TV ratings in its second series in 1995. Clooney crossed over to guest in popular sitcom *Friends* with *ER* co-star Noah Wyle in February 1995. Major film roles followed in 1996 with leads in *One Fine Day* and *From Dusk Till Dawn*.

RIGHT: Matthew Perry and Matt le Blanc in London to film the last episode of the current series of *Friends* which became one of the most popular sitcoms of all time. Marta Kauffman and David Crane began developing *Friends* under the title "Insomnia Cafe" in November 1993. After several script rewrites and changes, the series was finally named *Friends* and premiered on NBC's coveted Thursday 8:30 p.m. time-slot.

1995

Peter Schmeichel flies across the goalmouth to make another impressive save for Manchester United. Danish born Schmeichel was signed to the club in summer 1991 and was part of the Danish squad that won Euro 92, beating France in the final. He was voted The World's Best Goalkeeper in 1992 and again the following year, having helped United win their first League title for 26 years. In 1999 after seeing United win the treble and at the age of 36 he retired from English football to join Sporting CP in Lisbon.

OPPOSITE: Newly elected French President Jacques Chirac picks his way through a huge crowd of supporters as he arrives at his campaign headquarters in May 1995. He won the French presidential elections with 52 percent of the vote over his rival Socialist candidate Lionel Jospin. Chirac again stood for re-election in 2002, achieving a landslide victory against National Front candidate Jean-Marie Le Pen when voters chose Chirac to avoid Le Pen coming to power.

ABOVE: French president Jacques Chirac (left) and General Michel Guigon, military governor of Paris lead a mounted detachment of Republican Guards during the military parade on Bastille Day in the Champs Élysées, Paris. In 2002 Chirac survived an assassination attempt during the Bastille parade after a lone gunman associated with a violent far-right group was overpowered by bystanders.

1996

LEFT: Labour Party leader Tony Blair pictured with Newcastle United manager Kevin Keegan at an event designed to promote the 1996 European Football Championship which was staged in England.

OPPOSITE: After moving to Los Angeles in 1986, Brad Pitt took on a variety of jobs to pay for acting lessons. His film breakthrough came in 1991 when he appeared as the lanky cowboy JD in *Thelma and Louise*. Although on screen for only 14 minutes the character launched his career. Further successes followed, most notably, *Seven* and *Twelve Monkeys* in 1995, the latter earning him an Oscar nomination for Best Supporting Actor. Gwyneth Paltrow and Pitt were an item from 1994 to 1997 during which she played her breakthrough lead role in the big-screen dramatization of Jane Austen's novel, *Emma*.

RIGHT: Eric Cantona hugs Manchester United manager Alex Ferguson. After beginning his English football career with Leeds United, Cantona was signed to Manchester United in November 1992 for £1.2 million and was voted PFA Player of the Year in 1994. However, in 1995 Cantona kicked and punched a fan who was using threatening behavior and was given 120 hours of community service for the assault. Cantona captained United through the 1996-7 season and led the team to win the League title before retiring at the age of 30.

OPPOSITE: Having defeated Oliver McCall to claim the WBC world heavyweight title in 1995, Britain's Frank Bruno stepped into the ring in 1996 for a first title defense against American Mike Tyson. Held at the MGM Grand in Las Vegas, the bout was stopped after just three rounds, with Tyson securing victory on a technical knockout. The fight would prove to be Bruno's last professional encounter, whilst Tyson would be disqualified from his next match against Evander Holyfield, after biting both of his opponent's ears.

1996

Fans of the British rock sensation Oasis at the Knebworth Festival. In August, following in the footsteps of such rock and roll giants as Led Zeppelin, Queen, and the Rolling Stones, Oasis performed two outdoor concerts at Knebworth House in Hertfordshire, with a combined audience of more than 330,000; 2.6 million fans applied for tickets—a record demand in British rock history. Support was provided by The Prodigy, Ocean Colour Scene, The Charlatans, and Manic Street Preachers.

Britpop stars Oasis, pictured at Knebworth in August. In addition to their triumphant performances at the summer festival, the band won the Brit Award for Best British Album with their second album, *(What's the Story) Morning Glory?*, which spawned the massive hit singles, "Some Might Say," "Roll With It," "Wonderwall," "Don't Look Back in Anger," and "Champagne Supernova." This was also their breakthrough album in the US, providing them with their first *Billboard* Chart hits.

ABOVE: Alan Shearer squirts water into Paul Gascoigne's mouth, in celebration of Gazza's 79th-minute goal against Scotland, during the first round of the 1996 European Football Championships at Wembley. England won the game 2–0 but the England team would be knocked out at the semi-final stages, following a tense penalty shoot out against Germany, which left the score at 6–5.

OPPOSITE: Alan Shearer (right) celebrates England's opening goal of the competition against Switzerland with Darren Anderton.

LEFT: Spanish cycling star Miguel Indurain pictured at the 1996 Atlanta Olympics. From 1991 to 1995, Indurain won the Tour de France on five consecutive occasions, but, having suffered from a bout of bronchitis, in 1996 he lost out to Denmark's Bjarne Riis, who later admitted to having used the performance-enhancing drug Erythropoietin. Indurain shone at the Olympics, however, winning a gold medal in the individual time trial in the first year that professional cyclists were allowed to compete.

OPPOSITE: In 1996, 23-year-old Melissa Johnson became Wimbledon's first streaker, when she took to the Centre Court ahead of the men's singles final between MaliVai Washington and Richard Krajicek, wearing only an apron. Both players burst into laughter, as did most of the crowd. Washington drew further amusement by baring his own chest. Krajicek went on to win the match, becoming the only Dutch player to take the Wimbledon title. Johnson suffered no punitive action from the normally strait-laced club.

1996

ABOVE: German long-distance runner Uta Pippig crosses the finish line to secure victory in the 100th Boston Marathon, becoming the first woman to win the event on three consecutive occasions. Pippig was also hoping to win the marathon at the 1996 Summer Olympics in Atlanta, but having gone out fast to establish a convincing lead, she dropped back to eighth position, and was ultimately forced to drop out of the race, suffering from a stress fracture in her leg.

OPPOSITE: "The King of Swing," Pete Sampras, performs a crowd-pleasing shot between his legs during his opening match against Richey Reneberg at Wimbledon. Sampras had won the competition for three successive years, but in 1996 he would be knocked out in the quarter-finals stage by Richard Krajicek. Nevertheless, Sampras won the ATP Championship that year, and held on to the No.1 ranking for a consecutive 102 weeks between April 1996 and March 1998.

1996

Brazil's Mônica Rodrigues defends the net against Italy's Annamaria Solazzi during the women's beach volleyball at the Atlanta Summer Olympics. The sport first appeared at the Olympics as a demonstration event in Barcelona in 1992, but in 1996 it was introduced as an official Olympic sport for the first time. Rodrigues and her team-mate Adriana Samuel eventually took silver, while another Brazilian duo, Jackie Silva and Sandra Pires won gold.

Basketball legend Michael Jordan scores for the Chicago Bulls in their 106–101 victory over Orlando Magic, during the 1996 Eastern Conference Finals. Jordan had returned to the game the previous year, having briefly left the sport to play baseball with the Birmingham Barons and Scottsdale Scorpions, but he quickly made his presence felt, leading the Bulls to triumph in the 1996 NBA Finals against the Seattle SuperSonics, and ending the season with a record number of wins. Considered the finest basketball player of all time, Jordan's endorsement of sporting brands brought him great wealth, with Nike even designing the *Air* range in homage to the star.

An eight-year-old boy wields a Kalashnikov on the streets of Monrovia, Liberia as heavy fighting takes place around the city's main military barracks. Battles broke out between two warring factions as the Liberian Civil War, begun in 1989, continued to escalate; major battles took place between future president Charles Taylor, chief of the National Patriotic Front of Liberia (NPFL), and rival warlord Roosevelt Johnson. The city was severely damaged during the fighting; its displaced population included many homeless and orphaned children and youths drawn to the capital seeking refuge and support.

On the morning of June 15, 1996 the IRA detonated a bomb in Manchester, outside the Arndale Shopping Centre; the seventh attack since the group broke their ceasefire in February. Fortunately, due to a phone call warning of the attack, police were able to evacuate the immediate area. An attempt was made to defuse the 3,000lb device but the final blast, the largest known in peacetime Britain, caused widespread damage to the surrounding buildings estimated at £700 million. Despite attempts to clear the area over 200 people behind the police cordon were injured by the force of the blast and falling debris.

As rain stops play during the quarter final match between Pete Sampras and Richard Krajicek, Cliff Richard entertains the crowd by leading a sing-along at Wimbledon's Centre Court, accompanied by Virginia Wade, Pam Shriver, Gigi Fernandez and Conchita Martinez. His impromptu performance included renditions from his back catalogue such as "We're All Going On A Summer Holiday", "The Young Ones" and the appropriate "Singing In The Rain". The previous year, Richard became one of the first pop stars to be knighted.

ABOVE: Michael Johnson celebrates as he runs past the stadium clock showing his new world record of 19.32. Johnson shattered his previous record in the men's 200 meters at the Centennial Olympic Stadium during the Summer Olympic games in Atlanta. In his career Johnson won four Olympic gold medals and was crowned world champion eight times. His 200 meter time of 19.32 stood as a record for over 12 years. Johnson is the only male athlete in history to win both the 200 meter and 400 meter events at the same Olympics—a feat he accomplished at the Atlanta Games.

OPPOSITE: British sprinter Linford Christie, in action at the 1996 Summer Olympics in Atlanta. In 1992, Christie had won gold in the 100 meters at Barcelona, and was hoping for a medal in Atlanta, but despite making it through to the final, he was disqualified after two false starts. The race was won by Canada's Donovan Bailey, in a world record-breaking time of 9.84 seconds, and Christie officially retired from athletics the following year.

1996

The New York Yankees pile on top of each other after winning the World Series at their home ground, the Yankee Stadium in New York. The 1996 series matched defending champions and favorites, Atlanta Braves, against the Yankees. Despite losing their first two games, the Bronx Bombers went on to win the next four, finally defeating the Braves in the crucial show-down to win their first championship since 1978.

1996

318FT

92.3 K-ROCK

The Bronx Bombers continue their celebrations on the hallowed turf of the Yankee Stadium. Police formed a circle round the jubilant players as they became only the third team to lose the first two games at home and go on to capture the crown. Yankee manager Joe Torre and his team were later awarded the Major League Baseball Commissioner's Trophy by American League President Gene Budig.

1996

LEFT: Top vocal group Take That announce their breakup L-R Jason Orange, Gary Barlow, Mark Owen, and Howard Donald. Formed in Manchester in 1990, the band sold more than 25 million records between 1991–96. Take That's dance-oriented pop tunes and soulful ballads dominated the charts in the first half of the 1990s and they wowed audiences with their energetic stage routine. Pop maverick Robbie Williams had already left the original lineup in 1995 to pursue a solo career.

OPPOSITE: Despite announcing his retirement in 1992 with the No More Tours tour, by 1995 Ozzy Osbourne, had returned to performing and recording, and, shortly after co-headlining the Castle Donington festival with Kiss in 1996, he was to launch Ozzfest, a two-day rock festival which took place in Phoenix, Arizona, and Devore, California, featuring such bands as Slayer, Biohazard, and Fear Factory. Ozzfest subsequently evolved into an annual US tour, augmented by festival dates in the UK and Europe.

ABOVE: Serbian riot-police face down the ethnic Albanian protesters in Kosovo. At the heart of the conflict in Yugoslavia was a bitter racial divide between Serbs and ethnic Albanians, which led to ethnic cleansing on a large scale with great bloodshed and widespread displacement of civilian populations. While many share responsibility for the Kosovan disaster, Slobodan Milosevic was the grand architect and instigator of the war.

OPPOSITE: Kalashnikov in hand, a 16-year-old member of the Kosovo Liberation Army (KLA) stands in front of a car riddled with his bullets that killed the Serb policemen inside. After six years of Serbian oppression, many among Kosovo's Albanian population concluded that since peaceful protest had been ignored then armed aggression was the only way to restore previous levels of autonomy for the province. The KLA resistance militia was formed, launching attacks against Serbian security forces from April 1996.

1997

ABOVE: "Blair's Babes" pose with the new Prime Minister on the steps of Church House, Westminster. On May 1 the Labour Party swept to power with a landslide victory in the general election. The Conservative campaign had been hampered by infighting and accusations of corruption; in contrast, Tony Blair's invention of New Labour, combined with a slick campaign, saw a modernized socialist party secure more seats in Parliament than ever before. A record number of women MPs were elected, comprising almost one in four of Labour's successful candidates.

OPPOSITE: William Hague with his fiancée Ffion Jenkins. Hague was hosting a party to garner support in his campaign for the Conservative Party leadership. Kenneth Clarke secured the most votes in the first two rounds of the contest, but Hague won the third and final round to become the Opposition leader.

Prime Minister Tony Blair and US President Bill Clinton pictured in 10 Downing Street, during the President's one-day visit to Britain at the end of May. Throughout a morning of talks, the pair discussed foreign and economic policy, international approaches to employment, and the ongoing peace process in Northern Ireland, with President Clinton urging an end to all hostilities, calling on the IRA to participate in discussions, and to adopt an unconditional ceasefire.

Following an address to Tony Blair's Cabinet by Clinton, which was almost certainly the first of its kind since Nixon's 1969 meeting with Harold Wilson's Cabinet, Prime Minister Blair and President Clinton held a press conference in Downing Street's Rose Garden. The two men reiterated their commitment to the alliance, or "Special Relationship," between Britain and the United States, but beyond shared political values, there was also a clear personal bond between them.

1997

RIGHT: In 1996 up and coming British tennis player Tim Henman partnered Neil Broad to win a silver medal in the doubles event at the Atlanta Olympics as well as making it to the quarter-finals at Wimbledon before being knocked out by America's Todd Martin. In 1997 Henman again reached the Wimbledon quarter-finals, this time by defeating the defending champion Richard Krajicek in the fourth round. In the same year Henman also claimed his first ATP tournament victory in Sydney, Australia.

OPPOSITE: American actor George Clooney pictured at the Planet Hollywood Restaurant in London, alongside a life-size replica of his costume from the 1997 movie *Batman and Robin*. During the 1990s, Clooney was propelled to fame by the drama series *ER*, and gained his first major movie roles in *From Dusk Till Dawn*, *One Fine Day*, and *The Peacemaker*.

LEFT: Although the middle Sunday of the 13-day Wimbledon tournament is usually a rest day, in 1997 a run of disruptive bad weather forced play on that day. As a result, Wimbledon hosted a "People's Sunday," where show court seats were unreserved and available at lower than usual prices. As Tim Henman emerged onto No.1 Court for his match against Paul Haarhuis, former world number one John McEnroe led the fans in a Mexican wave.

OPPOSITE: Sixteen-year-old rising Russian tennis star Anna Kournikova in action in 1997. Kournikova had made her Grand Slam debut at the US Open the previous year, where she was defeated in the fourth round by world number one Steffi Graf. In 1997 however, Kournikova would make it to the semi-finals at Wimbledon, becoming only the second woman to do so in her debut outing at the tournament, the first being Chris Evert in 1972.

1997

LEFT: A former cross-country and middle-distance runner, the British athlete Steve Backley began his championship javelin career in 1987 at the European Junior Championships in Birmingham. Ten years later, he would win a silver medal at the World Championships in Athens, having previously broken two world records, as well as winning a bronze medal at the 1992 Olympic Games in Barcelona and a silver at the 1996 Olympics in Atlanta.

OPPOSITE: Streaker Nikki Moffat marks her appreciation for Tiger Woods in inimitable fashion at the 1997 British Open. Woods had only turned professional the previous year, but quickly captured both the public imagination and the attention of the golfing world. In 1997 he not only became the youngest ever Masters winner, but also won by a record 12 strokes, and went on to score victories in three further PGA tour events. Less than a year after his professional debut, Woods rose to the top of the world rankings and received the award for "PGA Player of the Year."

ABOVE: British tourists soak up the nightlife in Sant Antoni, on the Balearic Island of Ibiza. Popular as a haven for bohemians, hippies, and artists since the 1960s, by the 1990s Ibiza had become the destination of choice for young European revellers, with the island boasting some of the largest nightclubs in the world, and attracting some of the biggest DJs in the business. The local authorities also seemed remarkably tolerant of such hedonism, although reports in the British press were typically less favorable.

OPPOSITE: US sprinter Michael Johnson in action at Athens, where he would win gold in the 200 meters. The previous year, in Atlanta, Johnson had become the first man to win both the 200 and 400-meter races at the same Olympics, setting record times in both. In 1997 Johnson declared himself "the world's fastest man" leading in May to a highly publicized 150-meter race against Canadian sprinter Donovan Bailey at Toronto's SkyDome, which was won by Bailey when an injury forced Johnson to pull up short of the finish line.

ABOVE: U2's Bono and Adam Clayton, onstage during the band's 1997 PopMart tour. Earlier in the year, U2 had released their ninth studio LP, *Pop*, which contrary to its title, showcased a darker, more experimental sound than previous albums, with a more dance-orientated feel. The album hit the top of the charts in over 30 countries, including the UK and US.

OPPOSITE: Bono greets a fan from the stage. As with their previous Zoo TV tour, "PopMart" involved a highly complex stage set, which included a huge golden arch, massive video screens, and elaborate costumes, all of which were intended as ironic references to the excesses of both rock and roll and consumerism. The tour was one of the highest grossing of the year.

1997

RIGHT: Artist Marcus Harvey's "Myra," a portrait of the "moors murderer" Myra Hindley, which formed part of the "Sensation" exhibition at London's Royal Academy of Arts. The painting was seen as being particularly controversial due to the fact that it was created using the handprints of children, and had to be temporarily removed from display after a series of attacks by vandals. It was later returned to the gallery, protected by a sheet of glass.

OPPOSITE: Damien Hirst's "The Physical Impossibility of Death in the Mind of Someone Living," on display at the "Sensation" show. Comprised of a 14-feet-long tiger shark encased in a tank of formaldehyde solution, the piece was commissioned by Charles Saatchi in 1991, and became one of the most iconic works to emerge from the "Young British Artist" shows, which he sponsored in the 1990s. In addition to those by Hirst and Marcus Harvey, "Sensation" included works by such artists as Tracy Emin, Chris Ofili, Jenny Saville, and Jake and Dinos Chapman.

THE AMERICAN ASSOCIATES GALLERY

1997

OPPOSITE: Actor Robert Carlyle pictured in front of a poster for hit British comedy movie, *The Full Monty*, in which he plays Gaz, one of a group of unemployed Sheffield steelworkers who form a male striptease act, in the hope of lifting themselves out of poverty. The film won a BAFTA Award for Best Film in 1997, and was nominated for four Oscars, including Best Picture and Best Director. Those awards were ultimately claimed by James Cameron's massively successful *Titanic*, although *The Full Monty* won the Academy Award for Best Original Music Score.

RIGHT: The Red Cross brought the landmines issue to Princess Diana's attention and in January 1997 she made her first visit to Angola on their behalf. It was estimated there were 15 million mines throughout the country of 12 million inhabitants. Determined to bring the plight to the world's attention she worked with the Halo Trust, the mine clearance team, and very publicly walked through the middle of a half-cleared minefield in Cuito.

The handover ceremony on July 1, 1997 marked the transfer of Hong Kong, a British Crown Colony since 1842, to the People's Republic of China. The ceremony began at 6 P.M. on June 30 and ended at 8:30 P.M. the following day. Shortly before midnight the Union Flag was lowered over Government House and presented to the last British Governor of Hong Kong, Chris Patten. Among the dignitaries attending the ceremony were Prince Charles (representing the Queen), British Prime Minister Tony Blair and Foreign Secretary Robin Cook; from China, President Jiang Zemin and Premier, Li Peng. The new leader Tung Chee-hwa was sworn in as Hong Kong's Chief Executive. Shortly after midnight Prince Charles and Patten boarded the Royal Yacht *Britannia* and waved a final farewell, ending more than 150 years of British control.

British girl group the Spice Girls, performing at their first major international concert, in Istanbul, Turkey, in late 1997. Although formed in 1994, the Spice Girls first exploded onto the pop scene in mid-1996, with their debut single, "Wannabe," which became the first of six consecutive UK number one singles between 1996 and 1998; they included "Say You'll Be There," "2 Become 1," "Mama/Who Do You Think You Are," "Spice Up Your Life," and "Too Much." The band took advantage of their iconic status, and like The Beatles before them linked it to their Englishness, using the Union Jack in their shows and merchandizing. Shrewd manager Simon Fuller organized multi-million-dollar sponsorship deals for the girls—the Istanbul series, released on video as *Girl Power! Live in Istanbul* was part of their deal with Pepsi.

LEFT: Prince Naseem Hamed performs an impressive back flip following his victory over opponent Billy Hardy in the first round of his boxing match at the Nynex Arena in Manchester. The light-footed southpaw retained his IBF featherweight title after Hardy was caught by a right hook that broke his nose and his cheekbone and the fight was stopped after only 93 seconds.

OPPOSITE: Nelson Mandela shares a joke with Spice Girls Mel B (Scary Spice) and Geri Halliwell (Ginger Spice) at his official presidential residence, Mahlamba Nalopfu, in Pretoria, South Africa.

1997

ABOVE: Cars ablaze on the Antrim Road in Belfast, after rioting erupted following marches by the Northern Ireland loyalist Orange Order. Minor scuffles during the parades were followed by a number of more serious incidents of violence occurring afterwards. These included the shooting of soldiers, police and civilians, as well as bomb blasts in the Oldpark and Suffolk areas of the city. The nationalist paramilitary organization, the IRA, claimed responsibility for the attacks.

OPPOSITE: US President Bill Clinton's visit to London in May 1997 took place at the same time as his representative, Special US Envoy George Mitchell, was brokering talks between the opposing factions in Northern Ireland, a process begun by Clinton's own efforts since becoming President and now reaching critical mass. One of Tony Blair's first actions as Prime Minister was to endorse Mitchell's framework document which would culminate in the Good Friday Agreement in April 1998.

1997

The Hubble Space Telescope in orbit above the earth after its separation from the space shuttle *Discovery*. Named after the astronomer Edwin Hubble, the telescope is a highly versatile research tool and was first carried into orbit by a shuttle mission in April 1990. The telescope orbits outside the earth's atmosphere and so is able to take very sharp images of distant objects in the universe, which has led to many breakthroughs in astrophysics. Its design allows astronauts to service the telescope in space: a necessity from launch when a serious problem in the telescope's optics had to be repaired in the first service mission in 1993; further enhancements and repairs in the second service mission in 1997 enabled the telescope to transmit more and better data about deep space.

1997

OPPOSITE: Author J.K. Rowling with her first book *Harry Potter and the Philosopher's Stone*. The novel, written on an old manual typewriter, was finished in 1995 and finally published two years later by Bloomsbury Publishing in the UK and then by US publishers, Scholastic in 1998, who replaced "Philosopher's" with "Sorcerer's" in the title. Collecting many prizes along the way the book launched a seven-title series that would see her characters dominate family reading and cinema around the world for years to come, transforming the fortunes of Rowling and her publishers.

ABOVE: Celebrities Jill Dando, Sir Cliff Richard, and Gloria Hunniford visit the Hampton Court Flower Festival.

1997

Daily Mail

1961   1997

Britain mourned as Princess Diana's funeral cortège moved slowly through the streets of London. An estimated one million people lined the route as Diana's sons William and Harry accompanied by Prince Charles, the Duke of Edinburgh, and her brother Earl Spencer walked slowly behind the hearse. Millions more around the world watched the televised ceremonies of the day. Diana died in a car crash in Paris, along with friend Dodi Fayed and their driver, after trying to escape the paparazzi who were in pursuit of the couple. Mourners flocked to her London home, Kensington Palace, where a knee-deep sea of floral tributes grew by the hour (previous page). Diana was laid to rest on an island in the lake at the Spencer family estate, Althorp Park, Northamptonshire.

1997

The ocean liner *Titanic* in a dock scene from the movie written and directed by James Cameron. Starring Kate Winslet and Leonardo di Caprio the movie focused on an onboard romance between two young passengers who end up fighting for survival as the ship was sinks. Cameron began shooting footage of the actual wreck RMS *Titanic* in 1995 and the film was finally released in December 1997. At the time it was the most expensive film ever made with a budget of $200 million. It rapidly became a huge commercial success, the highest grossing movie of all time, while receiving high critical acclaim and winning eleven Academy Awards, including Best Picture and Best Director. The movie's soundtrack was also a hit, making Celine Dion's title song "My Heart Will Go On," the biggest-selling single of 1998 and a number one hit around the world.

1998

August 7: Firemen and helpers work to remove the bodies of people who died when a bomb exploded near the US embassy and a bank in Nairobi, Kenya, killing at least 60 people, including eight Americans, and leaving more than 1,000 injured. US ambassador Prudence Bushnell was slightly hurt in the blast, which reduced a six-story building to rubble. Another bomb exploded almost simultaneously in Dar es Salaam, Tanzania, killing six people.

1998

LEFT AND OPPOSITE: In March about 11,000 people joined a march from Hyde Park through the streets of central London in support of decriminalizing cannabis. Supporters from all over Europe took part in the demonstration that culminated in a rally in Trafalgar Square. The event was sponsored by *The Independent on Sunday* newspaper, which supported the medical use of cannabis for pain relief. MS sufferers led the march in wheelchairs. The rally brought strong opposition from anti-drug groups, who countered that cannabis is harmful to health and to society. The debate raged on either side of the Rally and focused on Home Secretary Jack Straw, whose son had been arrested for possession of the drug.

1998

RIGHT: Will Smith performing at a concert in 1998. Smith originally pursued a career in music until he was given a part in the sitcom *The Fresh Prince of Bel-Air*. This highly successful television series lasted for six years during which he began to be offered movie roles. The first, 1993's *Six Degrees of Separation*, was soon followed by the highly-acclaimed *Independence Day* (1996). He was cast as Agent J in the first of three *Men in Black* films in 1997.

OPPOSITE: Angolan President Jose Eduardo dos Santos welcomes South African President Nelson Mandela on a state visit in April 1998. Dos Santos, the leader of the MPLA, became President of Angola in 1979 after the death of Agostinho Neto. Angola achieved independence from Portugal in 1975 after a prolonged military struggle; there then followed a bloody civil war until 2002. The MPLA was supported by South Africa during this dark chapter and Nelson Mandela made achieving peace there a personal mission.

RIGHT: Citizens of Daira de Ramika on the outskirts of Relizane organize themselves for self-defence during the Algerian civil war which raged through most of the 1990s. Daira de Ramika and neighboring villages were attacked in January 1998, on the first day of Ramadan, just days after the massacre in nearby Sehanine; hundreds of civilians died at the hands of armed militants. From 1991, when military intervention ended the election hopes of the Islamic Salvation Front, a civil war broke out in which the population, already decimated by a war of independence from France, suffered further horrors.

ABOVE: A soldier stands in a tank in Oued Allel, 12 miles south of Algiers.

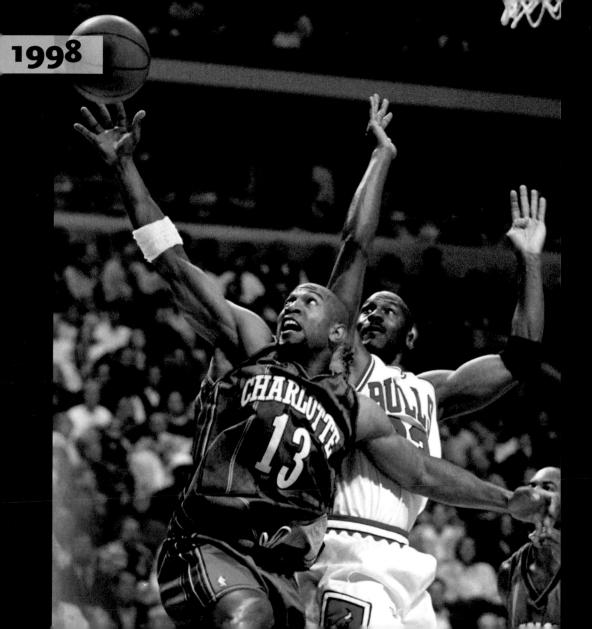
1998

RIGHT: British actor Ewan McGregor and his wife Eve. McGregor made his name in the international scene with his starring role in Danny Boyle's 1996 *Trainspotting*. More recently McGregor appeared in the glam rock movie *Velvet Goldmine*, which was nominated for a number of awards, including an Oscar and a BAFTA Oscar. In 1999 McGregor stepped into the shoes of Alec Guinness, playing a young Obi Wan Kenobi in the first prequel of the *Star Wars* saga.

OPPOSITE: Bobby Phills of the Charlotte Hornets attempts to grab a rebound from Michael Jordan of the Chicago Bulls, during the Eastern Conference semi-finals. The Hornets won game two of the series at the United Center in Chicago, but the Bulls were subsequently spurred into action, winning the next three games against the Hornets, and going on to win the Eastern Conference Championship after a challenging finals contest against the Indiana Pacers.

ABOVE: Scenes from the "Countryside March" in London's Hyde Park. The demonstration was organized by the Countryside Alliance, with over 250,000 protestors marching through the capital in support of a range of concerns, including the falling incomes of farmers, the public right to roam, and the development of green-field sites. Perhaps the largest single issue however, was that of fox hunting, which followed the publication of Labour MP Michael Foster's private member's bill to ban hunting with dogs.

OPPOSITE: Demonstrators pictured at the gates of the Russian Embassy in Kensington, London. Eight arrests were made after "bloody" handprints were daubed on the Embassy's entrance, in protest against the Russian bombing of the Chechen capital, Grozny. Following conflict with Russia between 1994 and 1996, Chechnya became increasingly lawless, with a massive surge in kidnappings and other terrorist activity, and open hostilities occurring between Islamist militants and the Chechen National Guard. As a result, the authorities in Grozny declared a state of emergency in 1998.

1998

LEFT: William Henderson takes a tumble in Super Bowl XXXII played on January 25 in San Diego. The American Football Conference champions Denver Broncos defeated the heavily favored National Football Conference champions Green Bay Packers 31–24. The Broncos' win was their first league championship after suffering four previous Super Bowl losses, and broke a 13-game losing streak for AFC teams in the Superbowl.

OPPOSITE: Bronco's running back Terrell Davis on his way to a winning touchdown.

1998

LEFT: Hollywood movie star Leonardo DiCaprio pictured attending a showing of his latest film, *The Man In The Iron Mask*. The movie also featured Gérard Depardieu, John Malkovich, Jeremy Irons, and Gabriel Byrne, and was another success, toppling DiCaprio's massive hit *Titanic* from its four month residence at the top of the US box office.

OPPOSITE: Julie Christie with Kate Winslet. Christie was nominated for Best Actress in a Lead Role in the 1997 Academy Awards for her role as Phyllis Mann in the Robert Altman produced film *Afterglow*.

1998

ABOVE: A policeman in shirt sleeves pictured in Notting Hill Gate, which has been transformed to winter for a scene in the movie *Notting Hill*. Despite posing numerous difficulties for the production team, much of the film was shot on location, with the exterior of screen writer Richard Curtis' own house featuring prominently, although the interior scenes were filmed at Shepperton Studios.

OPPOSITE: Hugh Grant and Julia Roberts filming *Notting Hill* on location in London's Portobello Road. Written by Richard Curtis, who had enjoyed huge success with *Four Weddings and a Funeral* in 1994, Notting Hill went on to become the highest-grossing British film of all time upon its release in 1999, and won a number of awards.

1998

LEFT: On May 13, just before the Queen and the Canadian Prime Minister, Jean Chrétien, were due to reopen Canada House in London's Trafalgar Square, three Greenpeace activists scaled Nelson's Column and unfurled a banner in protest against the destruction of Canada's temperate rainforest by logging companies. The campaign proved highly effective, with a number of major British companies agreeing to stop the purchase of Canadian timber and associated products until the felling of ancient woodland was halted.

OPPOSITE: Manchester United football star David Beckham and his Spice girl fiancée Victoria Adams on the day they announced their engagement.

1998

ABOVE: Children wave from a balcony during demonstrations in Sierra Leone. Following years of civil war, in 1997 the Armed Forces Revolutionary Council had overthrown President Kabbah's civilian government, and civilians were being shot and hacked to death by ARFC rebels in towns and villages across the country. High Commissioner Penfold was responsible for organizing the evacuation of hundreds of people from the capital Freetown, and worked closely with President Kabbah during his enforced exile in neighboring Guinea.

OPPOSITE: Demonstrations in Sierra Leone, in support of the British High Commissioner Peter Penfold, who had been recalled to London to face investigation over the "Arms to Africa Affair." Penfold was accused of acting contrary to British Government policy in recommending that Sierra Leone's President Kabbah should seek the support of the British company Sandline, which supplied arms and mercenaries to aid the overthrow of the military junta that had seized power in 1997.

1998

Scottish and Brazilian soccer fans descend upon Paris for the opening game of the 1998 FIFA World Cup. Around 60,000 Scots were estimated to have made the journey to the French capital, to bear witness to what promised to be one of the most prestigious and challenging matches faced by their national side. Some 20 years earlier, Scottish supporters had developed a reputation for hooliganism, but in 1998 journalists voted the "Tartan Army" as the best supporters at the World Cup.

Members of the Scotland team look on as Brazil celebrate their fourth-minute goal in the opening match of the World Cup. The South Americans took full advantage of a nervous start from Scotland, and having won a corner, César Sampaio scored with a powerful header from Rivaldo's curling ball. However, by half-time Scotland had equalized, with John Collins scoring from the penalty spot after Sampaio had brought down Kevin Gallacher.

ABOVE: The English World Cup squad fly home on Concorde sporting the flag of St. George. Despite playing against Argentina with 10 men after Beckham was sent off, goals from Owen and Shearer meant the game ended 2–2 but England lost the penalty shootout and were knocked out of the competition. The French hosts reached the final, playing against defending champions Brazil. Goals from Zidane and Petit gave France their first World Cup victory.

OPPOSITE: David Beckham is given a red card after kicking Diego Simeone during the game between England and Argentina in the second round of World Cup 98. Beckham first appeared in the national squad in 1996, just one season after joining Manchester United, and was promoted to the captaincy in 2000.

1998

Although originally designed in the 1980s for Cold War operations, the US Air Force's B-2 stealth bomber had its combat debut during Operation Allied Force in Kosovo and would see continued use during the ongoing wars in Iraq and Afghanistan.

1998

RIGHT: Dutch tennis pro Richard Krajicek was Wimbledon Men's Singles Champion in 1996. In 1998 Krajicek progressed to the semi-finals, where he would encounter Croatia's Goran Ivanisevic.

OPPOSITE: Pete Sampras went on to win his fifth Wimbledon title at the tournament, despatching Australia's Mark Philippoussis in the quarterfinals, Britain's Tim Henman in the semi-finals, and Croatia's Goran Ivanisevic in a fiercely contested final. Sampras ended the year as world number one for a record sixth consecutive year, and was also recognized as the ATP Player of the Year for a record sixth consecutive time. Henman meanwhile, had given his best performance at the Championship and entered the ATP top ten rankings for the first time.

ABOVE: The view of London's Millennium Dome and Canary Wharf, seen from the Thames Barrier flood defenses at Woolwich. The Dome project had been conceived under the previous Conservative government, but these plans were massively expanded, along with the budget, under Tony Blair. By 1998, much of the main structure was in place, including the distinctive domed roof, however, behind the scenes the cracks were already beginning to show, with the project's creative director, Stephen Bayley, resigning at the start of the year.

OPPOSITE: Serena Williams began the year ranked number 96 in the world and made her Grand Slam debut at the Australian Open, where she lost to her sister Venus in the second round.

ABOVE: Prime Minister Tony Blair, with deputy Prime Minister John Prescott and Jack Cunningham. Cunningham was appointed Minister to the Cabinet Office in Blair's 1998 cabinet reshuffle. Dubbed the "cabinet enforcer" by the press, Cunningham was tasked with coordinating party policy following severe criticisms over welfare reforms, spin doctoring, and a perceived split within the party between "Blairites" and supporters of Chancellor Gordon Brown.

OPPOSITE: James Major, the son of the former Prime Minister, and his fiancée, the model and presenter Emma Noble, enjoy being in the limelight while attending the premiere of the sci-fi disaster movie *Armageddon*, in London's Leicester Square.

ABOVE: Sean Connery and Catherine Zeta Jones pictured by the River Thames, during the filming of the movie *Entrapment*. Although Jones had been acting since childhood, she first came to prominence in the early 1990s as Mariette Larkin in the British TV adaptation of H.E. Bates' *The Darling Buds of May*, before gaining international recognition starring in the 1998 Hollywood swashbuckler *The Mask of Zorro*.

OPPOSITE: "Kopf," an artwork by German sculptor Stefan Hablützel, on show at Christies in London in December, where Charles Saatchi was selling some 130 works of modern art. The auction featured a range of pieces by both well-established and newly emergent artists, and included the creations of people such as Rachel Whiteread and Damien Hirst, whom Saatchi had sponsored as part of the recent Young British Artists scene.

1998

The Chicago Cubs play the St. Louis Cardinals on September 8 at Busch Stadium, St. Louis, Missouri. Mark McGwire of the St. Louis Cardinals hits a 341-feet line drive over the left field wall for his 62nd home run of the year, surpassing the 37-year-old record held by Roger Maris for the single season home run total. The Cardinals defeated the Cubs 6–3.

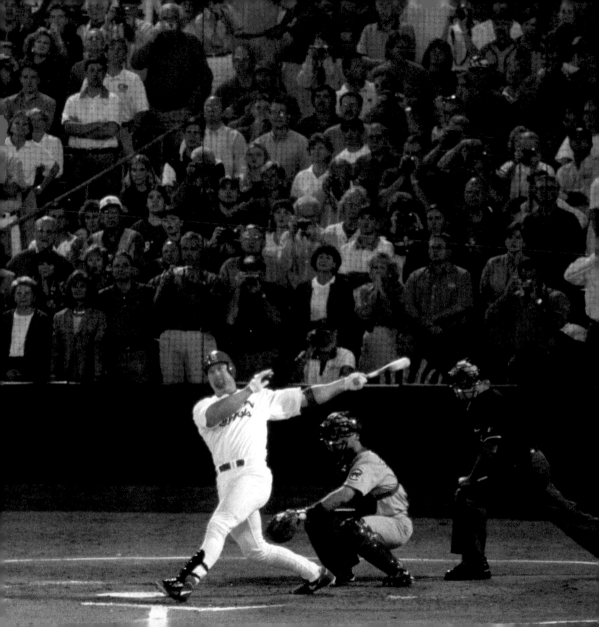

1998

RIGHT: A breakdancer demonstrates his skills ahead of the B-Boy Championships at London's Brixton Academy. Although very much a phenomenon of the 1980s, breakdancing experienced a resurgence during the 1990s, with the first championships being held at the Shepherds Bush Empire in 1996. The first two events attracted sell-out crowds of around 2,000 spectators, leading organizer Hooch to move to the Academy in 1998, where 5,000 fans came to watch dancers from around the world.

OPPOSITE: Moroccan middle-distance runner Hicham El Guerrouj wins the 1,500 meters at the IAAF Golden League Final, which was held at the Luzhniki Stadium in Moscow in September. Two months earlier, El Guerrouj had stunned the world with his performance at the Golden Gala athletics meeting in Rome, where he had shattered the world record of three minutes 27.37 seconds, which had been set by Algerian rival Noureddine Morceli some three years earlier.

1998

LEFT: Make up artist Gina Kane begins work on Robbie Williams, ahead of his "Jeans for Genes" charity launch. Following the success of his debut solo album the previous year, in 1998 Williams issued the follow-up *I've Been Expecting You*. The LP proved to be the singer's most successful, debuting at the top of the UK album charts and going on to sell around 5 million copies. It also spawned Robbie's first solo number one single, the John Barry-inspired "Millennium."

OPPOSITE: A model shows off one of Geri Halliwell's costumes during a charity auction at Sotheby's. The former Spice Girl was auctioning off her memorabilia in aid of the children's charity, Sargent Cancer Care. Lots included Geri's MGB Roadster and numerous extravagant stage costumes, and the sale raised a total of almost £150,000, with the star item proving to be her iconic Union Jack mini-dress, which was bought by the Hard Rock Hotel in Las Vegas, at a cost of over £40,000.

1998

ABOVE: Demonstrators on the streets of Peshawar burn effigies of US President Clinton, following a series of American cruise missile strikes on targets in Sudan and Afghanistan. These were launched in response to the terrorist bombings of the US embassies in Tanzania and Kenya, which were believed to have been carried out by Islamic extremists. However, the missile strikes in Sudan destroyed an important pharmaceutical plant, which had no proven links to terrorism.

OPPOSITE: "Eco warrior" Scottie, pictured at protest camp in Greenwood, Staffordshire. Following the establishment of the first road protest camp at Twyford Down in 1991, anti road building campaigns gathered momentum in Britain throughout the 1990s, with the largest being centered on the construction of the Newbury Bypass between 1995 and 1997.

ABOVE: Crowds of fans line the streets in anticipation of a special midnight release of the video of James Cameron's *Titanic* in late 1998. Earlier in the year, the movie had become the most successful film of all time at the box office, with worldwide receipts in excess of $1 billion. Sales of the video also went on to break numerous records.

OPPOSITE: Actress Kate Winslet pictured on location in India with her filmmaker husband Jim Threapleton, during the making of *Holy Smoke*. The couple met while filming *Hideous Kinky* in Morocco and were married soon afterwards. Having starred in the Hollywood blockbuster *Titanic* in 1997, *Hideous Kinky* was a far more modest affair, both in terms of its production costs and success, although Winslet received a number of favorable reviews for her performance.

ABOVE: An elated Naoko Takahashi crosses the finish line to win the women's marathon at the 13th Asian Games, which were held in Bangkok, Thailand, in December. Takahashi led the race from start to finish to complete the marathon in two hours 21 minutes and 47 seconds, setting a new record for her country, Japan, and shaving four seconds off the time that she had set earlier in the year on home turf at the Nagoya International Women's Marathon.

OPPOSITE: Grand Champion Sumo Wrestler Akebono takes the stage to "purge the venue of all evil" during the official opening ceremony of the XVIII Winter Olympic Games. The world's best athletes on snow and ice from a record 72 countries competed for 68 gold medals over 15 days.

1998

WORLD WIDE WEB

ABOVE: Tim Berners-Lee, founder of the World Wide Web, speaks at the Seventh International World Wide Web conference in Brisbane. Berners-Lee, a British scientist, first developed an idea to share information using the concept of hypertext when he was contracted to The European Organization for Nuclear Research (CERN) in Geneva in 1980. Nine years later, he proposed a further plan to join hypertext to the Internet, also developing the initial Web browser and server.

OPPOSITE: Opera star Luciano Pavarotti pictured on stage in Modena, Italy, with the Spice Girls, who joined the tenor for his "Pavarotti and Friends" charity concert. A foursome since the departure of "Ginger Spice," Geri Halliwell, just two weeks earlier, the girls performed their single "Stop," before Pavarotti took to the stage with them for a rendition of "Viva Forever." As a result of his charity work, Pavarotti was appointed a Messenger of Peace by the United Nations in 1998.

1998

RIGHT: The daughter of actor Jon Voight, Angelina Jolie trained in the theater was an international model and performed in music videos before breaking into the world of film. Her first major part was in *Hackers* (1995), but it was for her role in *Gia* (1998), that she caught the public's attention.

OPPOSITE: Actor Matt Damon in a scene from *Saving Private Ryan*, directed by Steven Spielberg and released in 1998. The movie was set during the invasion of the Normandy beaches towards the end of World War II and began with a graphic 25 minutes of action depicting the Omaha beachhead assault on June 6, 1944. Also starring Tom Hanks and Edward Burns, the movie received high critical acclaim, winning five Academy Awards and an Oscar for Best Director for Spielberg.

Michael Jordan, number 23, of the Chicago Bulls shoots over Karl Malone of the Utah Jazz during game six of the 1998 NBA Finals played on June 14, 1998 at the Delta Center in Salt Lake City. Chicago Bulls defeated Utah 87–86 and won the series 4–2.

ABOVE: *(L to R)* Director Quentin Tarantino, actress Frances Farmer, and actors John Travolta and Robert Duvall at the Eighth British Academy of Films and Television Arts Awards held in Beverly Hills, California. During the ceremony Travolta was honored for his contribution to the international entertainment industry, after starring in the films *Saturday Night Fever*, *Primary Colors*, and *Pulp Fiction* and his television work on the sitcom *Welcome Back Kotter*.

OPPOSITE: Hillary Clinton signs autographs for children during a visit to Lagan Meadows, Belfast. At home America's First Lady was closely involved in setting up several laws relating to the funding of children's healthcare and the systems for children needing foster care or adoption. However, 1998 was to be a stressful year for Hillary after allegations were made by a former White House intern who claimed she had an affair with Bill Clinton.

1999

At the Ndabezitha Homestead, Richmond, South Africa, young United Democratic Movement members take cover under fire from African National Congress assailants during a confrontation following the massacre of 11 members of the Ndabezitha family at their homestead on January 24, 1999. In 2001 five United Democratic Movement sympathizers were convicted for the revenge murders that followed the assassination of UDM regional leader Sifiso Nkabinda the day before the massacre. The African National Congress and the United Democratic Movement were in a bitter conflict that killed hundreds during the 1990s.

New Zealand-born Russell Crowe made his first film, *Romper Stomper,* in 1992, and was soon to catch America's eye. He was sought out by Sharon Stone for *The Quick and the Dead* (1995), but his first major hit was 1997's *LA Confidential.* In January 1999 shooting began on Ridley Scott's epic *Gladiator,* which received five Academy Awards, including Best Picture and Best Actor for Crowe.

Matt Damon, Jude Law, Gwyneth Paltrow, and Jack Davenport, stars of *The Talented Mr Ripley*, at the party which followed the film's premiere. The movie received five Academy Award nominations and was a showcase for the talent of these four young actors: although Damon and Paltrow were already Hollywood names, Law's role brought him star status; Davenport, would become better known outside his TV roles, playing character parts in such movies as *Pirates of the Caribbean*.

1999

In April 1999 the journalist and television presenter Jill Dando was brutally murdered with a single shot to the head, outside her front door in Fulham, London. Despite extensive work by the Metropolitan Police and widespread media coverage no suspect or motive for the crime could be found. Dando had fronted many programs including *Crimewatch* which led to much speculation about the motive for the killing. After two years local resident Barry George, who had a reputation for stalking local women was convicted and given life imprisonment. However, the evidence was deemed unreliable in subsequent appeals and he was released in 2008. Her murderer still remains at large.

1999

ABOVE: Kosovan refugees in Albania take to the River Drina to cool off in summer 1999. Hundreds of thousands of ethnic Albanians fled the province during the fighting.

OPPOSITE: In June 1999, after Slobodan Milosevic agreed to withdraw Serb forces from Kosovo, NATO's Kosovo Force, KFOR, was sent in to maintain peace and security. Here, British paratroopers cross the border from Macedonia into Kosovo.

1999

ABOVE: In October, Russian troops entered Chechnya with the intention of bringing it back under federal control. The capital Grozny was surrounded and besieged through the winter, with Russian forces finally gaining control in February the following year. Here Chechen women carry their belongings through the ruins of Grozny; civilian and military casualties were high in the fierce fighting.

OPPOSITE: Russian President Boris Yeltsin meets with his American counterpart, Bill Clinton, at an Organization for Security and Cooperation in Europe summit in Istanbul in November 1999. Russia's war in Chechnya topped the agenda of the summit, with Russia airing its frank views over NATO's intervention in Kosovo.

ABOVE: Australian troops applaud as the 2nd Battalion Royal Gurkhas end their tour of duty in East Timor and prepare to return to barracks in Brunei. The Gurkhas were among the first UN troops to arrive following the outbreak of violence.

OPPOSITE: US President Bill Clinton and the French President Jacques Chirac pictured at the Royal Palace in Amman, where they were paying their respects to King Hussein of Jordan, who had died of Cancer aged 63, bringing an end to his 46-year reign. Clinton was just one of four generations of US leaders present, with George H.W. Bush, Jimmy Carter, and Gerald Ford all in attendance at the ceremony, in addition to numerous world leaders and other dignitaries, including the Syrian President Hafez al-Assad, Israel's Prime Minister Binyamin Netanyahu, and Palestinian leader Yasser Arafat.

1999

Teresa Weatherspoon, number 11 of the New York Liberty, shoots from half court to beat the Houston Comets in game 2 of the 1999 WNBA Finals at the Compaq Center in Houston, Texas, on September 4, 1999. The WNBA has been the butt of many jokes over the years, but in 1999 Weatherspoon's amazing shot proved that women had skills on the court, too. The shot gave New York a game 2 win, 68–67, forcing the WNBA finals to a game 3, which unfortunately the Liberty went on to lose.

LEFT: A sculpture by the Anglo-French artist Pierre Vivant. The work of art, constructed from over 70 sets of custom-made traffic lights, took six months to make. Vivant's traffic-light tree replaced a dying plane tree that had to be removed.

OPPOSITE: A refugee camp at Cambambe outside the city of Caxito, Angola, January 1999. Despite the efforts of a UN peacekeeping force and the provisions of the Lusaka Protocol during the mid-1990s, the civil war continued to rage in Angola from 1975 until 2002. The legacy of the war was a humanitarian catastrophe with over 4 million people displaced, the cultural impact of 10,000 impressed child soldiers, and the residue of 15 million land-mines sown during the war.

General Auguste Pinochet, former head of state of Chile, came to London for treatment in 1998. A Spanish judge issued an international warrant for Pinochet's arrest for crimes against Spanish citizens which the UK government enforced, placing Pinochet under house arrest while considering what course of action should be taken. Human rights protesters campaigned through 1999 for the full force of the law to be applied to the elderly Pinochet. Eventually he was allowed to return to Chile to face justice in his own country. Thanks to laws of immunity protecting politicians, Pinochet avoided prosecution, dying before he could be convicted.

Serb protesters demand an end to the NATO aerial bombing of targets in Yugoslavia. Known as Operation Allied Force, the bombing campaign was designed to damage the Serbian military infrastructure and other strategic targets, with the ultimate aim of forcing the withdrawal of military and paramilitary troops from Kosovo. The British Foreign Secretary, Robin Cook, was singled out for criticism by protesters, having defended NATO's involvement in the conflict. Although it created negative reaction, the NATO policy proved successful in halting aggression in Kosovo.

1999

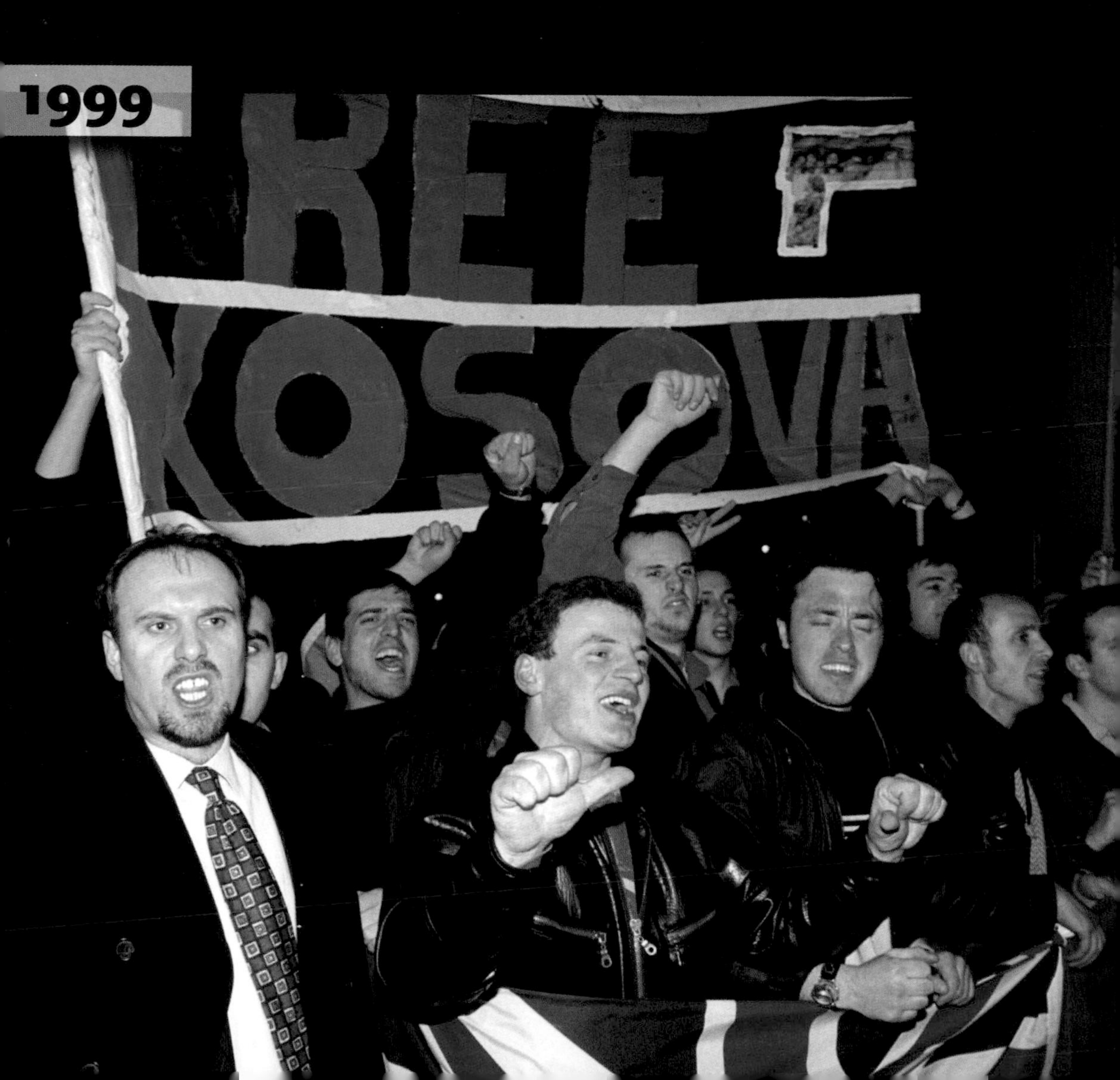

ABOVE: Antony Gormley's *Field for the British Isles* on display in Colchester, Essex. The sculptor's original *Field* was made with the assistance of a family of brickmakers in Mexico in 1991, following which the artist has overseen the creation of a series of different versions around the globe, with versions being made in Brazil, Sweden, the People's Republic of China, and Japan.

OPPOSITE: Albanian demonstrators march in support of NATO air strikes against the Serbs. Following the abolition of Kosovo's autonomous status within Serbia, tensions in the region increased dramatically, with conflict erupting as ethnic Albanian paramilitaries belonging to the Kosovo Liberation Army began to put up armed resistance to the Serbian and Yugoslavian forces that they saw as their oppressors. The NATO bombing campaign began in March 1999, and would persist until June.

1999

The selection committee of the Royal
Academy summer exhibition sits in
judgement. Every year since 1769 the
institution has held an annual exhibition of
art. Initially restricted to works by the Royal
Academicians themselves, by the 1990s
it had become the largest open exhibition
in Britain, with around a thousand works
being selected from several thousand
entries. In addition, the Academicians
continued to exhibit their own works, with
David Hockney and Peter Blake being two
of the most notable participants in 1999.

1999

ABOVE: Protestors participating in the Global Carnival Against Capital in London on June 18, set off a fire hydrant outside the London International Financial Futures Exchange. The day of protest, which became known as J18, began with a peaceful march, although the use of horses and CS sprays by police led to outbreaks of sporadic violence as crowds were forced out of the City of London; only 16 arrests were made on the day.

OPPOSITE: British anti-euro protestors pictured demonstrating outside Mansion House, the official residence of the Lord Mayor of the City of London. The euro was adopted as the currency of participating nations at midnight on January 1, 1999, although the physical notes and coins of these countries would remain legal tender for two further years. The initial 11 countries comprising the "Eurozone" were Austria, Belgium, Finland, France, Germany, Ireland, Italy, Luxembourg, the Netherlands, Portugal, and Spain.

Students run from Columbine High School as police try to provide cover. On April 20, 1999, in the small suburban town of Littleton, Colorado, two high-school seniors, Dylan Klebold and Eric Harris, enacted an all-out assault on Columbine High School during the middle of the school day. The two masked teenagers embarked on their murderous massacre by storming the school and blasting fellow students with guns and explosives before turning the weapons on themselves in their planned suicide mission. When the day was done the alienated and angry young men had killed 12 fellow students and one teacher in their deadly attack.

1999

An Australian peacekeeper passes a burning building in Dili, the East Timorese capital. Also known as Timor-Leste, the country was released from annexation by Indonesia in 1999, becoming independent once more. Fighting broke out when militias who wanted East Timor to remain a province of Indonesia used force to promote their views. The peacekeeping force drove the militias back into the Indonesian section of the island of Timor but violence continued up to 2008.

ABOVE: In 1999, the US scored a double victory at Wimbledon, with Lindsay Davenport and Pete Sampras winning the singles championships. It was the third consecutive year that Sampras had claimed the Wimbledon title, and his sixth overall. Sampras ended the year as world number one for six years in a row, but following Wimbledon he was forced to withdraw from a number of tournaments because of a serious back problem, allowing Wimbledon runner-up Andre Agassi to capture the title.

OPPOSITE: Tiger Woods in the rough at Carnoustie Golf Links, Scotland, during the 128th British Open Golf Championship. Although Woods eventually tied for seventh place in the event, alongside David Frost and Davis Love, 1999 was a remarkable year for the golfer, during which he scored eight wins, including the Memorial Tournament, the PGA Championship and the Tour Championship. As a result, Woods was named PGA Tour Player of the Year and also the Associated Press Male Athlete of the Year.

1999

RIGHT: A frustrated Jean Van De Velde pictured in the Barry Burn at the 18th during the British Open at Carnoustie. Having performed strongly during the second half of the event, Van De Velde seemed poised for victory, but despite a three-stroke lead, events conspired to bring about a three-man playoff against Paul Lawrie and Justin Leonard. Lawrie went on to win the championship, coming back from 10 strokes down, in the biggest comeback ever witnessed at the British Open.

OPPOSITE: The solar eclipse is viewed above the Millennium Dome in London. On August 11, 1999, Britain experienced its first total solar eclipse since 1927, with the moon's shadow traversing the Atlantic Ocean to make first landfall in Cornwall, before crossing parts of central Europe and Asia, and ending in the Bay of Bengal off the coast of India. At the time, this total solar eclipse was believed to have been viewed by more people than any other in history.

1999

RIGHT: Top triple-jumper Jonathan Edwards launches himself through the air during the qualifying rounds at the Seville World Athletics Championships. The world record holder added a bronze to his comprehensive medal collection. His extraordinary achievements have earned him a place in history as one of the world's greatest and most loved athletes. In 2002 he would hold gold medals for the four major competitions—Olympics, World Championships, Commonwealth Games, and European Championships.

OPPOSITE: Britain's Denise Lewis' third and final long jump in the women's heptathlon during the IAAF World Athletics Championships in Seville. The talented all-round athlete went on to take the silver medal after finishing 137 points behind rival Eunice Barber.

1999

LEFT:British distance runner, Paula Radcliffe recovers on the track after finishing second in the 10,000 meters final at the seventh World Athletics Championships in Seville. The rangy athlete missed out on her quest for gold by a few seconds after Ethiopian Gete Wami unleashed a lethal sprint over the final 200 meters. Earlier in the year the head-bobbing Radcliffe had won the 5,000 meters at the European Cup in Paris

ABOVE: An easy going and popular individual off the track, Radcliffe's steely determination manifests itself in her ruthless and tough approach in competition.

1999

ABOVE: In the tradition of other Irish boy bands, Dublin's Westlife was discovered by pop impresario Louis Walsh and signed to RCA by Simon Cowell. The quintet released their first single In March 1999, "Swear It Again," which immediately topped the charts in Ireland and the UK. The band is the only act in UK history to have its first seven singles go straight to Number one.

OPPOSITE: World record holder Colin Jackson drapes himself in the Welsh and Union flags after winning gold in the 110 metre hurdles at the Seville World Athletics Championships. After a disappointing Olympics in 1996, many doubted that Jackson would be able to repeat his World Championship win of 1993 but Jackson produced his best time of the year dipping on the line to defeat Cuba's Anier Garcia.

1999

The Millennium Wheel was floated up the River Thames in sections for assembly before being raised into position in two stages. The innovative structure, dubbed the "London Eye," is the tallest cantilevered observation wheel in the world, rising high above the city skyline at 443 feet tall. The construction has 32 capsules, representing the 32 boroughs of London, which turn to give spectacular panoramic views of the city—you can see around 25 miles from the top on a clear day.

ABOVE: On the last day of the English football season Manchester United beat Tottenham 2–1 to win the Premiership title; a week later they defeated Newcastle United to take the FA Cup. In tense final moments of the European Cup in Barcelona, United took the title with a 2-1 win against Bayern Munich. Their unique treble win earned the team a heroes' welcome.

OPPOSITE: Chicago Cubs right-fielder Sammy Sosa swings on his 60th home run of the season, hit in the sixth inning of the game against the Milwaukee Brewers in Chicago's Wrigley Field on September 18. Sosa, who had 66 home runs in the 1999 season, became the first player to hit 60 home runs in two seasons after an exciting 1998, when he competed with Cardinals' Mark McGwire for the home runs record, beating McGwire to the 60 mark but then being overtaken by McGwire, who reached 70 in the 1998 season.

ABOVE: Enfant terrible of the Young British Artists movement, Damien Hirst, poses in his studio. The controversial artist is best known for his spin and spot paintings, medicine cabinet sculptures, and glass tank installations. His 14-foot tiger shark immersed in formaldehyde became the iconic image of British art in the 1990s.

OPPOSITE: Antony Gormley with a model of his Quantum Cloud sculpture commissioned for a site next to the Millennium Dome in London. The elliptical cloud structure seen here in development, is to be formed from five-feet lengths of randomly oriented steel which envelopes a 65-feet-high human body form at the center.

1999

Colin Montgomerie lines up for a putt on the 16th green at the 1999 British Open Golf Championship at Carnoustie in Scotland. Local lad, Scotsman Paul Lawrie claimed the Claret Jug after winning a four-hole playoff over 1997 Open Champion Justin Leonard, and Jean Van de Velde. The unfortunate Frenchman had suffered a calamitous collapse after coming to the last hole with a three-shot lead. His unpredictable play landed his ball in the Barry Burn, the water hazard in front of the green, and he ended the round with a triple-bogey 7, in one of the most infamous final-hole meltdowns in modern golf history.

1999

OPPOSITE: Protesters urge China to hold talks with the Dalai Lama, the spiritual leader of Tibetan Buddhists, at a "Free Tibet" demonstration in front of the Hyde Park Hotel during the state visit of Chinese President Jiang Zemin in October 1999. The dissidents were campaigning against the Chinese occupation of Tibet.

ABOVE: A guardsman races after a protesting Tibetan activist as he runs toward the carriage carrying Chinese President Jiang Zemin and Queen Elizabeth II in the Mall in central London during the Asian leader's state visit to the UK.

LEFT: Australia on their way to a convincing victory 35–12 over France in the Rugby World Cup championship final at The Millennium Stadium, Cardiff on November 6, 1999. The sporting world had high hopes that a team from the northern hemisphere could break the southern hemisphere's stranglehold, but it was not to be as the Wallabies received the cup for the second time in the tournament's four-season history.

OPPOSITE: Britney Spears' debut single "...Baby One More Time" peaked at number one in the *Billboard* Hot 100 for two weeks in January 1999. When it was released in the UK, the 18-year-old's catchy single went straight to number one and became the top-selling single of 1999. Spears' unabashed sexy schoolgirl act raised eyebrows in the older generation but re-popularized teen pop, launching Britney on a carousel career that would bring fame, wealth, and notoriety.

1999

Texan marvel Lance Armstrong races
through Paris in the final stage of the

1999

RIGHT: Mike McCann, keeper of the Great Clock of Westminster, watches the celebrated timepiece as the seconds count down towards the dawn of the new millennium. Along with horological engineer, Brian Tipper, he was to spend the last hours of the 20th century in the mechanism room ensuring that Big Ben's 140-year-old works ring in the new year smoothly.

OPPOSITE: Pierce Brosnan and girlfriend, American TV journalist Keely Shaye Smith, arrive at the premiere of the latest James Bond movie, *The World is Not Enough*, the 19th film in the series of 007 movies, and the third to star Pierce Brosnan as the fictional MI6 agent. The movie has the longest pre-title opening sequence of any Bond movie and culminates in a boat chase on the River Thames that features MI6's actual HQ.

During an impeachment trial prompted by the Lewinsky sex scandal, presided over by Chief Justice William Rehnquist (center rear), the United States Senate votes on articles of impeachment and acquits President Clinton on February 12, 1999. Fifty-five senators voted not guilty and forty-five voted guilty on Article I—perjury before a grand jury—and on Article II, 50 senators voted guilty and 50 senators voted not guilty. A two-thirds majority of 67 votes was necessary to remove the president from office. Republican house managers sit at the curved table, left, while at the right sits the President's defence team, including Chief White House Counsel Charles Ruff (in wheelchair) and, next to him, White House Special Counsel Greg Craig.

Keanu Reeves and Hugo Weaving fly toward each other in a scene from the science-fiction movie *The Matrix*. Directed by the Wachowski brothers it was the first of the Matrix series of films, animation and comic books. The movie was renowned for its use of "bullet time" as a visual effect and subsequently won three Academy Awards for Visual Effects, Sound Design, and Film Editing.

1999

LEFT: The wives of the United States team line up at the Country Club in Brookline, Massachusetts for the opening ceremony of the 1999 Ryder Cup. The American team were criticized for moments of poor etiquette during the match when they were overcome with enthusiasm for "the most impressive come-from-behind victory" in the Cup's history.

OPPOSITE: "Posh and Becks"–Spice Girl Victoria Adams and England football player David Beckham, pictured leaving her parents' Hertfordshire home, as the couple headed to Ireland for their wedding. They were married at Luttrellstown Castle on July 4, following which a lavish reception was held, at an estimated cost of some £500,000. An exclusive photograph deal with *OK!* magazine ensured that much of the media was kept at bay, although some pictures were inevitably leaked to the press.

1999

The crew of Mission STS-103 prepare for the launch of the space shuttle Discovery, scheduled for December 19, 1999. Their objective was further repair to the Hubble telescope. Originally planned for June the following year the mission was brought forward as six of the telescope's gyroscopes were beginning to fail. Other adjustments included replacement of the computer and the outer insulation..

Crew members Michael Foale (l) and Claude Nicolier work from the robot arm to remove the old on-board computer from the Hubble space telescope to replace it. This was the second of three planned six-hour space walks. The mission finally returned to earth on December 27 having reached an altitude of 378 miles, the highest shuttle orbit on record, and having covered a journey distance of 3.25 million miles.

1999

LEFT: President Clinton and his wife Hillary visit the Stenkovec refugee camp in Macedonia. During the Kosovo War in 1999 an estimated 360,000 ethnic Albanian refugees poured into the country from Kosovo in an attempt to reach safety. Serbian forces had begun a campaign of ethnic cleansing and Nato had launched a series of attacks in Serbia and Kosovo. The Serbs were eventually driven out in the summer and the United Nations took over Kosovo's administration. The province finally declared its independence in February 2008.

OPPOSITE: The clock tower at the Palace of Westminster is illuminated by fireworks as Big Ben chimes midnight on Millennium Night, New Year's Eve, 1999. London celebrated the millennium by setting off a "river of fire" with pyrotechnics extending along the Thames from Tower Bridge to Vauxhall Bridge, followed by a firework display, launched from a series of barges along the river, as well as opening the Millennium Dome.

ACKNOWLEDGMENTS

Written and edited by:
Tim Hill; Gareth Thomas; Murray Mahon; Marie Clayton; Duncan Hill; Jane Benn; Alison Gauntlett; Alice Hill

****

The photographs in this book are from the archives of the Daily Mail. Thanks to all the photographers who have contributed and the film and television companies who have provided Associated Newspapers with promotional stills.
Every effort has been made to correctly credit photographs provided. In case of inaccuracies or errors we will be happy to correct them in future printings of this book.

Thanks to all the staff at Associated Newspapers who have made this book possible. Particular thanks to Alan Pinnock.
Thanks also to Steve Torrington, Dave Sheppard and Brian Jackson.

Thanks to the many Associated Newspapers photographers who have contributed including:
Darryn Lyons, Alan Davidson, Jim Hutchison, Craig Hibbert, David Crump, Barry Beattie, Glenn Copus, Ted Blackbrow, Jenny Goodall, Steve Poole, Steve Back, Mark Allan, Philip Ide, Keith Waldegrave, Clive Limpkin, Barry Phillips, Mike Forster, Murray Sanders, Johnson/Liaison, David O'Neill, Frank Tewkesbury, Mike Floyd, David Parker, Ian Richards, Rogers, Srdja Djukanovic, Kevin Holt, Darren Heath, Mike Hollist, Andy Hooper, Michael Thomas, Colin Davey, Nick Skinner, Mark Large, Jamie Wiseman, Alan Lewis, Mark Beltran, Louis Hollingsbee, Dave Shopland, Scot Staff, Mark Lloyd, Dieter Ludwig, Rob McMillan, Titus Pengelly, Clive Howes, F. Tewkesbury, Jeremy Selwyn, David Bennett, Russell Clisby, K. Towner, J. Minihan, Alex Lentati, D. Jones, Nick Cornish, Oliver Lim, Nigel Howard, Denis Jones, Paul Reed, Steve Waters, John Lillington,
With contributions from associated photographers: Gilles Leimdorfer, David Longstreath, Parick Downs, Pascal Guyot, Pat Benic, Ken Lennox, Francoise De Mulder, Saurabh Das, Michael E Samojadan, Gennady Galperin, Eric Feferberg, Corbis, Chris Bacon, Menahem Kahana, Wally Santana, Bob Collier, John Giles, Timothy Clary, Bob Galbraith, Harold Crawford, Mike Blake, Srdjan Ilic, Geraint Lewis, Peter Andrews, Jeff Haynes, Koji Sasahara, White House Photo, Itar-Tass, Manuel De Almeida, Ed Wray, Sue Ogrocki,

Published by Transatlantic Press
First published in 2010

Transatlantic Press
38 Copthorne Road
Croxley Green, Hertfordshire
WD3 4AQ

© Atlantic Publishing
For photograph copyrights see pages 382–3

A catalogue record for this book is available from the British Library.

ISBN 978-1-907176-03-6

Printed in China